OPPORTUNITIES IN
THE MACHINE TRADES

John A. Bell
Lonny D. Garvey

Foreword by
Matthew B. Coffey
President
National Tooling and Machining Association

Published in cooperation with the
National Tooling & Machining Association.

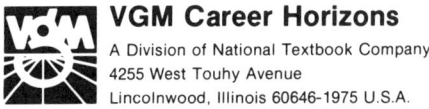

VGM Career Horizons
A Division of National Textbook Company
4255 West Touhy Avenue
Lincolnwood, Illinois 60646-1975 U.S.A.

Photo Credits
Front cover: upper left, National Tooling & Machine Assn.; upper right, Republic Airlines, Inc.; lower left and right, NTC.
Back cover: all, NTC.

1988 Printing

Copyright © 1986 by National Textbook Company
4255 West Touhy Avenue
Lincolnwood (Chicago), Illinois 60646-1975 U.S.A.
All rights reserved. No part of this book may
be reproduced, stored in a retrieval system, or
transmitted in any form or by any means, electronic,
mechanical, photocopying, recording or otherwise,
without the prior permission of National Textbook Company.
Manufactured in the United States of America.
Library of Congress Catalog Number: 86-060147

7 8 9 0 ML 9 8 7 6 5 4 3 2 1

ABOUT THE AUTHORS

John A. Bell has been employed by the National Tooling and Machining Association (NTMA) headquartered in the metropolitan Washington, D.C. area, since 1965. He is currently Manager of Training Activities. He manages one of the largest nation-wide pre-employment training programs with funding from the United States Department of Labor. From 1964 through 1985, over 17,000 persons have started training for metalworking careers under this massive NTMA-operated program.

NTMA is a non-profit trade association, which represents nearly 4,000 metalworking plants across the country, who employ skilled toolmakers, diemakers, moldmakers, machinists, and other metalworking occupational specialists. NTMA publishes a wide array of specialized textbooks and other training materials to help train people for rewarding metalworking career opportunities.

Jack did his undergraduate college work at Georgetown University and after completing active duty military service in 1954, he secured a graduate degree from American University. He works closely on all training activities with the 65 NTMA local chapters across the country. He acts as industry liason with the Bureau of Apprenticeship and Training, U.S. Department of Labor, as well as many states' apprenticeship agencies.

Lonny D. Garvey is currently Field Training Manager and Industry Coordinator for the National Tooling and Machining Association (NTMA). He supervises all field operations for the Association's pre-employment training program. He also works closely with the local NTMA chapter apprenticeship committees to establish and improve apprenticeship training programs.

Before decorated military service in Vietnam, Lon completed a tool and die apprenticeship program in Belding, Michigan. After his military service, he obtained an undergraduate degree at Ferris State College, and a graduate degree at Central Michigan University.

Prior to his current NTMA employment, Lon was the machine tool program instructional manager at Kellogg Community College in Battle Creek, Michigan.

He developed special open-entry/open-exit competency based training materials while at Kellogg. With NTMA, he is continuing the development of unique modular training materials for the training of skilled metalworkers. Those materials are now being used successfully in a wide variety of secondary and postsecondary schools, as well as many industry-sponsored metalworking training programs.

ACKNOWLEDGMENT

John A. Bell and Lonny D. Garvey wish to acknowledge the invaluable contribution of Benjamin J. Stern, whose earlier editions provided the basis for revision of this widely acclaimed book on careers in the machining trades.

FOREWORD

If you are mechanically inclined; if you like creative, challenging work; if you like to fix things, take them apart, and put them back together; if you like using your mind, and your hands to build things; then you might have the aptitude for one of several jobs with almost unlimited futures in the metalworking or machine trades.

Skilled machinists, toolmakers, diemakers, and moldmakers use sophisticated machine tools to cut and form metal with extreme precision to make the special tools, machines, and machined parts essential for all manufactured products. Their work is challenging. They use the latest manufacturing technology everyday.

If you are thinking about your career, and the points mentioned above apply to you, there are several things you should do to organize your plans. Take the initiative to evaluate the interest and the skills you now possess. Take a good battery of aptitude tests first. Include mechanical ability, mathematical concepts, and spacial relationships in the test battery.

If the test results are encouraging, then talk to a school guidance or career counselor, or a machine shop instructor, and ask them to help you visit a local tooling or machining plant so you can talk to the owner or plant manager. If you state your interest and reasons persuasively, they will help you.

The metalworking trades offer many outstanding career opportunities for those who can meet the qualifications. Maybe you have those qualifications. If so, a fascinating job in an industry often called the keystone of America's sophisticated manufacturing production system might be in your future.

If you are still in secondary school, take as many science, math, and mechanical lab classes as possible. Those courses will help you get a head start. Most postsecondary vocational/technical schools or community colleges, in or near industrialized areas, offer metalworking courses. These schools will help you acquire additional basic skills necessary to succeed in the metalworking trades.

If a metalworking career interests you, go for it! Good luck—ample opportunities are there for those who are qualified and aggressive enough to seek them out.

Matthew B. Coffey, President
National Tooling and Machining Association

CONTENTS

About the Authors..iii
Acknowledgments...v
Foreword...vi

1. **The Scope of the Machining Trades**............... 1
   What is a machinist? Historical sketch. Current needs and future outlook. Requirements for success. How the machinist is paid. Women in the machine shop trades. Summary.

2. **Machine Shop Operations**........................... 31
   Machinist all-around. Toolmaker. Diemaker. Tool and diemaker. Moldmaker. Instrument maker. Numerical control (NC) machine operator. Computer numerical control (CNC) machine operator. Electrical discharge machine (EDM) operator. Engine lathe hand or operator. Milling machine hand or operator. Drill press hand or operator. Cylindrical grinding machine hand or operator. Screw

machine hand or operator. Assembler or bench hand. Inspector. Layout person. The future of the machine shop.

3. How to Become a Machinist.......................... 59
What is apprenticeship? Apprenticeship legislation. The value of an apprenticeship. Apprenticeship programs. How do you get started? Federal and state training assistance. Veterans training programs. If you are under 18 years old. Stay in school. Puzzled about your future? Adding it all up.

4. Employment and Advancement..................... 89
Interviews. Civil service. Advancement. Other industries. Front office. Designing. Large machinery. Demonstrating and selling.

5. Related Fields..115
Becoming an engineer or technician. Teaching. Self-employment.

Appendix A: Recommended Reading....................133

Appendix B: United States Civil Service Regions.......135

Appendix C: U.S. Department of Labor Bureau of Apprenticeship and Training Regional Offices and State Offices..137

Appendix D: State Apprenticeship Agencies............144

Appendix E: Professional Societies, National and Local Trade Associations, and Labor Unions........148

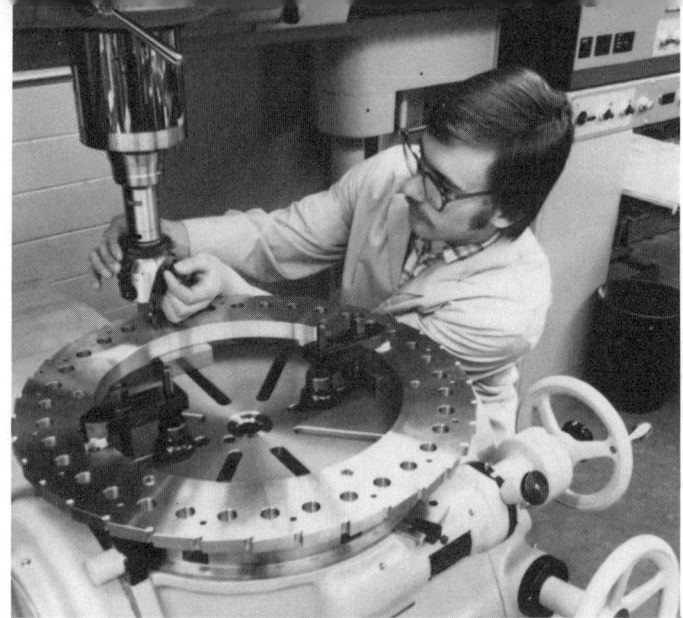

Above, a toolmaker makes final adjustments to the boring head of this jig bore. Tolerance of five millionths of an inch can be maintained with this ultra-precision machine. Below, an inspector makes notes about the stripper mechanism on the lower half of a 10-station die used in making beverage pull-up can tops. Photos: above, Remmele Engineering, Inc., and National Tooling and Machining Association; below NTMA.

CHAPTER 1

THE SCOPE OF THE MACHINE TRADES

He who hath a trade, hath an estate.
                              Benjamin Franklin

Skilled machinists are crucial to the mass production manufacturing system. Virtually all manufactured products which we use in our everyday lives depend on the skills of precision machinists at some point during their production.

The United States owes much of its present-day power and wealth to the use of machinery and mass production techniques by industry. When our nation was founded, all machines and all products were essentially hand made. One person made all the parts and then assembled them, adapting and modifying where necessary to make the individual parts fit and work together. That same person generally applied the finishing touches, the paint or varnish, or decorative embellishment, so that each item was actually an individual work of art—one of a kind.

The industrial revolution dramatically changed the social and economic formats for the world. Extensive mechanization of production systems shifted manufacturing from a home-or-cottage-type industry to a large-scale factory system.

In 1798, Eli Whitney, already famous for his invention of the cotton gin, developed the first standardized manufacturing process. He had contracted with the United States government to produce 10,000 muskets. To do so, he developed the first assembly line manufacturing system, based upon the use of uniform, interchangeable parts. In doing so, he became the world's first tool and die maker, and laid the foundation for our present mass production system. Many people say that Whitney was the inventor of mass production.

The word "tool" used in this sense does not mean hammers, saws or screwdrivers. A "tool" is any device that is used in holding, forming or shaping a material so that hundreds or thousands or even millions of identical parts can be produced, to the specific size and configuration required by the product design or blueprint. In order to make these tools, the toolmaker uses many machines and measuring instruments.

With the invention of the steam engine, and later the internal combustion engine, people recognized the tremendous advantages of mechanical power as compared to animal or human power. Once the first hand made automobile was invented, many people wanted one. To meet this new demand, and to reduce costs so that an even greater demand could be created, Henry Ford, and later his contemporaries, began to produce automobiles for the national market with assembly line production techniques far beyond anything Eli Whitney could have envisioned.

Yet it was Whitney's original concept, with its special tools for mass producing identical, interchangeable parts, that made it all possible. "Tooling up" became a part of our vocabulary, and the making of tools and dies became an industry in its own right, serving not only the auto manufacturers, but all other industries which quickly adopted the new and faster manufacturing techniques. Mass production was here to stay!

Many people famous in American industry and business were toolmakers, diemakers and machinists. For example, Walter P. Chrysler started his career as a machinist at age 17, and later founded and headed one of the largest automobile manufacturing companies in the United States. James Watt, a machinist and instrument maker, is renowned for his innovative designs for steam engines which could produce cheap and abundant power. George Westinghouse also began as a machinist and is recognized for many inventions which had significant influence on the American standard of living. The Wright brothers, machinists and bicycle makers, taught themselves the principles of aerodynamics and went on to make the first successful flights in a heavier-than-air craft. The Reuther brothers, both toolmakers, pioneered labor-management relations which led to the establishment of one of the early effective labor unions in the automotive field.

Because of these men, and many others whose genius fueled the tremendous manufacturing growth, Americans have and continue to enjoy one of the highest standards of living in the world. We thrive in an environment of growth and opportunity which results, primarily, from our enormous and sophisticated system of mass production and mass merchandising.

Machinist's training has proven, in countless cases, to be but the preliminary step to careers in many manufacturing fields. Thousands have spent challenging and interesting lives as machinists, helping our country achieve and maintain its preeminent status.

Frequently the tooling and machining industry is called the "Keystone of Mass Production." By using machines to mass produce items such as automobiles, hospital beds, computers—virtually all manufactured products—America's standard of living has become the envy of the world.

Our entire economy is based upon production. Few nations have ever attained as high a living standard as ours. America's genius for mass production of goods has resulted in comparatively lower costs to consumers.

The Scope of the Machine Trades 5

The basis of this high productivity is the machine. In every corner and facet of our lives, our work is done by machines—from the sophisticated kitchen food processor which slices, dices and blends our food; to the mammoth machines and transfer mechanisms which turn out our automobiles.

These machines must be both built and maintained; it is the machinist who does just that. Other highly skilled machinists, called toolmakers and diemakers, build the jigs, fixtures, and dies that produce the interchangeable parts which are the basis of our mass production. Again, it is the machinist who makes cutters and tools, and lathes, and other machines that cut, form, shape and process metals. Wherever machinery exists or is needed, machinists are present in one capacity or another—from the auto service center where they may be grinding camshafts or turning down armatures to the sewing machine plant or the linotype shop where they may be maintaining the machinery.

The machinist is a key factor in our industrial life. Even though our production machinery is becoming more automatic, thus requiring less attendant manpower, these complex mechanisms require additional and higher skilled personnel to build and maintain them. Teams of highly skilled toolmakers built many of the incredibly intricate parts and components for the first atom bombs. Present experiments in space travel, space satellites, rockets, atomic power, jet engines, gas turbines, environmental controls, guided missiles, and other weapons are even newer areas challenging the skilled machinist.

This book will define the work and duties of the various branches of the machining trades. Shop and work conditions, rates of pay, the status of the unions and their impact, and other aspects of labor conditions will be explained. Preparation for entry into the trade, methods of starting, opportunities for advancement, and the relationship of the machinist to other fields and to society as a whole will also be discussed. Other sources of information will be indicated as well.

WHAT IS A MACHINIST?

Hopefully, by this time you have begun to wonder just what a machinist is. Of course, you have heard the term used, but the chances are that you have never really given it much thought or had its meaning spelled out. You might say that a machinist is a skilled mechanic who uses a variety of machines and tools to shape metals of all kinds and other non-metallic materials into thousands of forms and sizes. Perhaps you have used a hacksaw to cut a piece of metal or maybe used a file to smooth it down. If you have, then you have done some of the work of a machinist. But when producing articles of cast iron, steel, bronze, aluminum, steel alloys, magnesium, and other materials to precise shapes and measurements, those hand tools are not adequate. Skilled machinists need many kinds of machinery. They use lathes, milling machines, grinders, drill presses, computer controlled machines and many other high-tech machine tools. Mechanics who can use all of these machines and hand tools with facility, read blueprints, handle shop mathematics, heat-treat steel, and use measuring instruments to work to very fine dimensions, are called all-around machinists. Sometimes this classification is graded into first class and second class. After years of experience and when they have learned to work with precise accuracy, machinists can become toolmakers, diemakers, and/or mold makers.

If, however, a mechanic concentrates on just one machine to the point of specialization, he or she becomes a lathe hand or operator, a milling machine hand or operator, or a grinder hand or operator. They could specialize in filing, scraping, fitting, assembling, and the like and thus become a bench hand, an assembler, or a fitter hand.

Here we must make a distinction between those often highly skilled specialists and the machine operator, an attendant whose function is to keep an automatic machine tool loaded and to make sure the finished piece goes on its way. These operators usually are employed in large, high production shops like automobile plants. However, somebody else must get these automatic and semiautomatic machines ready or set-up for production, grind and set the tools, instruct the operator, and make sure the work comes out to measurements. This person is called a *set-up person.*

Another highly skilled group of mechanics are the *instrument makers.* They not only have an all-around mechanical ability, in the same class as the toolmakers, but also a good technical background. In working with scientists, inventors, and experimenters, they must be able to translate their ideas into working models from sketches, diagrams, and verbal instructions. Instrument makers must be able to work with very little supervision.

Many shops employ *inspectors,* highly skilled in the use of measuring instruments, to supervise all the work going through and make sure that all measurements are up to specifications.

In addition to all these traditional trade categories, new and specialized jobs have arisen as a result of the widespread use of machine tools with electronically controlled, automatic cycle devices known as *numerical controls.* This technology has spread rapidly with a corresponding rise in job opportunities. Other new machine tools have been introduced which do not use the traditional methods of cutting and shaping metals but rely on electrical discharges and chemical action. These tools require special techniques in set-up and operation.

Another departure from the conventional methods of metal working is the introduction of the laser beam.

Powerful laser beams (concentrated light rays), set up in a machine tool can cut holes and shapes to exact specifications. Guided by computerized control circuitry, the operation can be entirely automatic and form part of a production line. There are many advantages from the use of laser beams, for example, the edges of the holes and shapes thus produced can be used with no further machining.

The *Dictionary of Occupational Titles,* published by the U.S. Department of Labor, describes a machinist thusly:

> Machinist, all around: sets up and operates a variety of machine tools and fits and assembles parts to fabricate or repair machine tools and maintain industrial tools, applying knowledge of mechanics, shop mathematics, metal properties, layout and machinery procedures. Observes and listens to operating machines or equipment to diagnose malfunction and determines need for adjustment or repair, studies blueprint, sketch, machine part or specifications to determine type and dimensions of metal stock surfaces, using such measuring and marking devices as calibrated ruler, micrometer, calipers. Uses machine tools such as lathe, milling machine, borer, grinder, drill press and hand tools such as scraper and files and such measuring devices as veniers, height gauge, and gauge blocks.

There are other specialized jobs in machine shops, but the ones mentioned on the preceding pages are the ones usually meant when the overall term *machinist* is used. Later in this book we will analyze these jobs more thoroughly. But first, suppose we talk a bit about the historical background of the machine trades.

HISTORICAL SKETCH

Human beings are natural toolmakers. We could never have survived our primitive beginnings with only our puny muscular strength to rely on. Somewhere in the past, one of our ancestors picked up a stone and tied a stick to it or sharpened a piece of flint to use as a knife and thus created tools. With these and other extensions of our natural powers, we could survive and make progress that was marked by tools and machines which became increasingly complex as we learned more about the laws of nature. Of course, it was only when we discovered and began to use metals like copper and iron and their alloys that our real ingenuity as toolmakers became apparent.

By the Middle Ages, there already existed a large body of knowledge in the fashioning of metals. The mechanics of Europe, Asia, Africa, and other parts of the world could work iron and steel to make the finest swords and weapons as well as body armor for the warriors. Metal workers knew enough of the laws of physics and mechanics to build machines for pumping water, milling flour, cutting and forging metals, printing books, and besieging fortified castles and cities. Machine tools, like the lathe and the drill, had been used for centuries although in primitive forms. What was lacking, however, was cheap power in large and dependable amounts. The only power available was generated by slaves or animals or provided by capricious winds and falling water.

A most instructive and interesting survey of the industrial world of eighteenth century Europe is provided by the great *French Encyclopedia of the Trades, Crafts and Industries* of that period. The eminent French philosopher, Denis Diderot, took twenty-five years to complete this work which consists of thirteen large folios or books. They contain drawings, diagrams, engravings, pictures and descriptions illustrating practices and procedures in such trades as metalworking, cannon founding and finishing, weaving of textiles, printing, cabinet-making, masonry and many others commonly practiced in France at the time. These illustrations show graphically the trade practices which transformed raw materials into finished and usable products. For the machinist, most interesting would be the engravings showing the mechanics of the day as they proceeded step by step in their work, as in the casting and finishing of cannons, and the diagrams of the machine tools of the day. The thirteen original volumes of Diderot's encyclopedia have been published in this country but condensed into three folios which can be seen in many of the larger libraries of our country.

By the eighteenth century, an industrial revolution was well on its way in England and parts of continental Europe that was to transform societies whose economies were based on agriculture into highly industrialized communities by the end of the nineteenth century. Many basic inventions such as the spinning Jenny and the automatic weaving loom in the textile industries led to the beginnings of the factory and manufacturing systems we know today. All this created a growing demand for cheap, dependable and plentiful power which the crude, low-powered and undependable steam engines of the early days could not supply. In Scotland and England a machinist named James Watt (1736-1819) turned his attention to this problem. Watt was an inventive genius, an instrument maker with several inventions to his credit, whose devices were used by the very active astronomers and scientists of the day.

Watt created several devices for the steam engine which solved the problem of a power source. He added a steam condenser; made the engine into a double-acting one in which the piston was driven back and forth by the steam and by ingenious valving; transformed this action into a rotary one; added a regulator to the valves; added a governor to regulate steam flow and to provide a safety measure; and by solving these problems, designed an improved boiler.

With these and several other ideas, he finally arrived at a safe, dependable, powerful steam engine which was the main source of power for the industrialized world until well into the twentieth century when the steam turbine and the internal combustion engine took over.

While Watt had solved the technical problems of a workable and dependable steam engine, his greatest difficulty now lay in getting the parts of the engine machined so that they would fit and work together. For example, the crude machine tools of the day could not cut or bore the large steam cylinder of Watt's engine round and close enough to prevent steam under pressure from escaping past the piston which was supposed to move within the cylinder.

At this point John Wilkinson (1728-1808), the greatest iron master and metal worker in England at that time, came to Watt's aid by developing and building a boring machine that did the job sufficiently well to make the steam engine workable. In James Watt's own words:

> Mr. Wilkinson has improved the art of boring cylinders so that I promise upon a 72" diameter cylinder being not further apart from absolute truth than the thickness of a sixpence in the most part.

It was this marvelous advance in heavy machine tool technique which transformed Watt's designs to a practical reality, and laid the solid foundation for the great industrial changes of the next century. Furthermore, as happens often in the history of human progress, Wilkinson's improved boring machine was followed by a torrent of inventions and improvements that completely transformed the machine tools and measuring devices of the day.

The modern, versatile king of machine tools, the lathe, began to emerge from its ancient form. The milling machine was invented, drill presses were improved, grinders came into being, the turret lathe was invented and improved, the metal planer appeared and a host of other machines and devices were added to the machine shop. In addition, measuring became more precise with the invention of the micrometer, the vernier, the height gauge and many other precision measuring devices. Finally, with the appearance of the practical dynamo and motor, an electrogenerator was hitched to the steam engine and our modern machine age began.

Thus, with the advent of cheap, almost unlimited, and dependable power, a complete revolution began not only in production methods but also in the field of metal working. Machine tools were rapidly improved and new ones invented. Consequently, by the close of the nineteenth century, there was in the United States a large body of journeymen machinists, proud of their trade and restless—often moving from job to job according to their moods. Among them were many specimens of that marvel of human skill and ingenuity, the

"Yankee Mechanic." The emergence of the automobile, the springboard by which many of these mechanics rose to fame and fortune, provided further impetus.

These skilled mechanics of the late nineteenth century and early twentieth century esteemed their crafts. Contemporary accounts tell us that the toolmaker of seventy-five years ago was the king of the shop and he bore himself like one.

> They wore top hats and frock coats to work, carried gloves and walking sticks. They didn't wear these while they worked—but they wore 'em on the street to show they were proud of their profession...on the job they wore a dinky white apron...in the old shops, the row of pictures of men in top hats in the front hall of the shop wasn't of the board of directors—it was of the toolmakers, and was a guarantee of ability... Remember, that a good man doesn't have to get all dirtied up to prove he's working.*

The twentieth century has been the age of discovery. Machinists now have at their command undreamed-of facilities, such as electrical power and controls, hydraulic devices, electronics, automatic machine tools using numerical controls, carboloy cutting tools, and others, all of which have provided them with marvelous new machine tools, measuring devices, steels, metals, and plastics. The one-eighth of an inch accuracy of which

---
*American Machinist, March 17, 1952, p. 151.

James Watt boasted now has given way to measurements often held to ten thousandths of an inch and even closer. The skills of machinists have kept pace with the progress of science and invention. The scope of their job opportunities has been widened immeasurably. New, formerly undreamed of metals are being alloyed to challenge their skills. New, almost fantastic devices are being designed daily to challenge their ingenuity.

CURRENT NEEDS AND FUTURE OUTLOOK

Since 1917, we have lived through two world wars, a "Boom-Bust" era in between, an interim of intensified "cold war," and disastrous undeclared wars in Korea and Vietnam. All the events of the twentieth century have helped generate an unprecedented "energy crisis," rampant inflation, and intermittent economic recessions. With all these crises, our nation must maintain a policy of total rearmament with new, more sophisticated weapons and nuclear deterrents, and support for large armed forces here and abroad. Other factors affecting future prospects for the machinist have been the rapid and spectacular emergence of space technology, rising concern for the control of environmental and ecological changes and conditions, and the search for new forms and sources of energy.

This last item has emerged as perhaps the most important and vital issue facing our country today. The events of the past several years have brought home in the most dramatic and troublesome fashion our complete dependence on imported fossil fuels and derivatives of crude oil such as gasoline. Our entire economic life has become dependent upon this. When the flow from the oil-producing nations is interrupted, we feel the effects immediately. As a result a search for alternate forms of energy and power sources has been launched with the recent adoption by Congress of a multibillion dollar program for developing synthetic fuels. These may be liquids and gases made from coal, or from shale rock or tar sands as well as heavy oils. They also include fuels made from organic materials such as the garbage collected from communities. This will mean the building of plants, the design and manufacturing of machinery and equipment, and other activities in which the machinist will have a vital role. In addition to all this, other forms of energy production are being explored, such as that derived from the sun and the wind.

One needs but to look at our automotive industry to note the effects of the phenomenal rise in gasoline prices as a result of ever-increasing costs of imported crude oil. The car makers have had to change over to the manufacture of smaller and smaller cars in order to improve mileage ratings. This vast multibillion dollar redesigning and retooling effort has affected the machine tool industry in particular, for it is obvious that skilled machinists must play an important role in these developments.

Despite fluctuating economic conditions, the demand for skilled machinists seems to be constant, and the future employment picture looks promising. There is a shortage of qualified applicants for jobs as toolmakers, diemakers, mold makers and machinists. Of course, this shortage will vary from one area to another. Even in periods of high unemployment, there still persists a need for skilled people in certain crafts and occupations, particularly those in metal-working. Skilled mechanics enjoy the benefits of increased job security.

The future demand for machinists will be affected by two main factors. As population and income rise, so too will the demand for such goods as automobiles, household appliances, and other industrial products, all requiring the machinists' skills. Partially offsetting this, however, will be worker productivity increases resulting from technological advances.

Chief among these advances is the expanding use of numerical and computer controls, which may greatly simplify the job of many machining workers and increase their efficiency. Additionally, more sophisticated applications of numerically controlled machine tools will require operators of greater skill and knowledge.

The last sentence of the preceding paragraph has particular significance. A great deal is heard today about automation and computerized devices that some predict might replace human hands in our factories and plants. What is often forgotten in all these predictions, however, is that it will take an increasing number of skilled hands to make and maintain these devices. In all this activity, the machinist will be a key figure.

There still exists a great diversity of all-round and specialized skills in the machine shop trades. Just examine the classified ads in any newspaper, you will always see appeals for the following categories of skilled machinists: lathe hands, milling machine hands, jig borer operators, gear cutter operators, automatic screw machine hands, set-up persons for various operations, turret lathe hands, assemblers, all-round machinists, numerical control machine operators, tool and die makers, mold makers, radial drill operators, and inspectors. Good hourly salaries will be offered, with plenty of overtime. Again it should be pointed out that while automation of machine operations may be spreading it would seem that skilled machinists of all kinds will probably be in demand for a long time to come.

In the words of Jack Kleinoder, former President of the National Tooling and Machining Association, and a very successful tooling and machining plant owner now retired, "It is a sobering fact to all industry that no matter how far we go with automatic production, tools and dies cannot be built by a pushbutton; the creative abilities of the tool and diemaker will always be needed."

The U.S. Department of Labor annual Occupational Outlook Handbook (1982-83 Edition) reports in 1981 an estimated 303,000 all-around machinists, 1,020,000 machine tool operators, 166,000 tool and die makers, 4,300 instrument makers, and 93,000 set-up persons in the United States. They were employed mostly in the metal manufacturing industry—making machine tools, special machinery, automatic production machines, and transportation vehicles of all types including automobiles—and wherever metal and other materials were bent, shaped, cut, formed, and otherwise fabricated. Many thousands were employed in nonmetal working industries such as the repair and maintenance shops or factories producing textiles, paper, glass and chemicals. Many others were employed as maintenance workers in a variety of factories and plants. A small number worked in research laboratories, model making shops, and the like.

REQUIREMENTS FOR SUCCESS

Before going into a detailed discussion of the various machine shop trades, it might be best to consider the general factors necessary for success in the field and also the general working conditions found in the shops.

If we were to select the most important personality trait for persons working in the machine shop trades, it might be a genuine liking for working with tools and machinery and for making and repairing all kinds of devices. If you possess this as well as a certain amount of manual dexterity, then you can confidently consider a career in a machine shop. Of course, you must also be able to tolerate dirt, grease, noise, and certain other so-called unpleasant aspects of workaday life. It is true that modern shops are usually comparatively clean and well-lighted and have adequate working and sanitation facilities. Still, a certain amount of dirt and noise is unavoidable. If you shrink from getting your hands and clothes dirty and greasy and from occasional scratches, burns, and bruises, then perhaps a machine shop is no place for you.

You also need to be in good physical shape—a sound body, good eyesight, and plenty of stamina. On many jobs you may have to stand all day; others may require lifting of tools, equipment, and metal parts. For close work with fine precision measuring instruments you will be using your eyes constantly. Of course, it is true that, given the proper spirit and incentive, handicapped persons also can become good machinists. If you are handicapped, however, give serious thought to your career choice and be sure to get the advice of medical and technical experts.

HOW THE MACHINIST IS PAID

As a rule, machine shop employees are paid on an hourly basis. The rate may vary from area to area and between beginners and journey persons. The table in this section (page 23) gives a general indication of the range of wages in 1985.

All work over an agreed minimum of usually forty hours per week is paid on a time-and-one-half basis. Almost all machinists enjoy pensions, paid vacations, paid holidays, and paid sick leave.

Although most employers pay machinists on an hourly basis, some plants, especially those engaged in mass production, may have supplemental piecerate incentives. This method guarantees a worker is given an incentive to produce more by being paid additional money for anything produced over a preset minimum.

It would be interesting and informative at this point to indicate just what fringe benefits a machine shop worker can expect nowadays. A check of want ads in various newspapers discloses the following fringe benefits advertised: paid vacations, a certain number of paid days off (holidays, personal leaves, birthdays, and others), family dental and medical insurance, pensions, sick leave with pay, free eyeglasses, bereavement leave with pay, cost of living adjustment every six months, profit sharing plan, and other benefits unique to indi-

AVERAGE STRAIGHT TIME HOURLY EARNINGS IN THE MACHINE TRADES
1985

	Machinist All-Around	NC Machine Operator	Die Maker
Atlanta, Georgia	8.97	8.48	11.92
Chicago, Illinois	10.27	10.94	13.15
Dayton, Ohio	9.58	9.48	11.57
Nashville, Tennessee	11.25	8.93	12.42
Detroit, Michigan	11.34	10.38	12.35
Denver, Colorado	10.58	8.50	11.40
Hartford, Connecticut	9.28	8.83	10.56
Houston, Texas	11.60	10.68	11.58
Orlando, Florida	8.62	5.50	8.00
Minneapolis, Minnesota	10.16	9.66	11.16
Milwaukee, Wisconsin	10.47	11.82	12.97
Newark, New Jersey	10.69	10.37	12.04
Long Island, New York	10.15	8.02	12.02
Pittsburgh, Pennsylvania	9.03	8.21	11.10
Portland, Oregon	12.02	13.19	15.19
Los Angeles, California	12.00	10.42	14.15
San Jose, California	13.82	9.07	19.43
St. Louis, Missouri	13.61	11.00	14.51
Toledo, Ohio	10.79	13.63	12.02
Phoenix, Arizona	10.71	9.49	12.38
Boston, Massachusetts	10.18	8.61	11.25
Philadelphia, Pennsylvania	9.84	9.13	11.95

NOTE: The above hourly wages are averages and are subject to changes resulting from economic conditions and new union-management contracts.

*Annual Area Wage Survey, National Tooling & Machining Association, Washington, D.C.

vidual shops. Of course, while many of these items are specified in union contracts, most will be offered by the predominant proportion of companies in order to attract and keep adequately skilled help.

Things were quite different when the author obtained his first job as a shaper hand in a large machine shop. Hours of work were fifty-four per week—ten hours a day Monday through Friday, and four on Saturday. Beginning wages were twenty cents per hour. There were no fringe benefits of any kind. One got paid for hours worked—and that was all. There was no worker's compensation—if one got hurt it was just too bad. Conditions for the worker have certainly improved dramatically!

In figuring wages, always keep in mind the difference between the indicated rates and take-home pay. Do not forget that wage deductions are usually made for unemployment insurance, social security (old-age benefits), sickness and accident benefits, federal income tax payments, as well as for other purposes designated by local laws.

The more highly skilled the worker, the better her or his chances of avoiding unemployment. Some industries have seasonal layoffs. Usually, the most skilled people are kept on. As far as the present and immediate future are concerned, however, skilled machinists need not worry about finding jobs.

WOMEN IN THE MACHINE TRADES

The machine shop trades have traditionally been dominated by men. Until 1917, during World War I, women rarely worked in this field. At that time the manpower shortages created by the drafting of millions of men into the armed services opened the way for women into many semiskilled and skilled occupations; they proved themselves competent and productive. Women operated every sort of machine in the machine shops and worked on the bench, on assemblies, or as inspectors. However, when the war ended and the men returned, these women were phased out, gradually disappearing from the shops. The same situation occurred during World War II in 1941-45. Over 6.7 million women were recruited and trained to fill a variety of vacancies in the nation's machine shops. For example, at the Boeing Aviation Corporation in Seattle, Washington, 45 percent of the production workers were women. Boeing had designed and was producing the B-17, the famous Flying Fortress, which proved to be the backbone of our air force. When World War II ended, the women were let go; but they had again proven that they could do competent work in the skilled trades.

The following excerpt from *The New York Times* (October 19th, 1979) clearly illustrates how things have changed since World War II:

TOKYO (AP) An experiment begun last year by Yamaha Motor Co. to operate a motorbike factory with women workers has proved a roaring success.

With some degree of apprehension, women were put on the assembly lines, as one official said, "to make better use of women-power."

He said the women had won the admiration of their male colleagues when the all-woman factory produced 175,000 minibikes last year, 25,000 more than initially planned.

"They are making ladies' bikes so it makes sense that ladies should build them," said overseas department spokesman Hitoshi Ishida.

Another reason may be that women are considered skillful at precision work.

When the experiment was launched in January 1977, the company management feared productivity would drop if only women operated the factory. Their fears have proved groundless and there are now plans to increase the number of female workers, Ishida said.

The factory started with 70 women but this has increased to 120, he said.

At present the factory is geared toward the domestic market and there are plans to put the women on larger and more powerful bikes in the future, Ishida said.

In 1964 the Federal Civil Rights Act became law. This landmark legislation, enforced by the Federal Equal Opportunity Commission and by local agencies, forbids discrimination in jobs on the basis of sex, race, or creed. This Act assured women of equal opportunities to enter any occupation they chose. Coupled with this law was the Federal Equal Pay Act of 1963 which required equal pay for equal work. As a result, there has been a marked tendency for women to get into the skilled trades.

In 1960 the U.S. Census Bureau reported there were 6,685 women in various machine trades occupations. By 1970 this number had increased to 11,787, representing a growth of almost 80 percent. In 1978, the *Statistical Abstract of the United States,* published by the Census Bureau, reported there were about 15,000 women machinists plus 3100 women toolmakers.

While these numbers are but a small percentage of the total workers in the field, women do seem to have an increasing desire to get into machine shops, and the opportunities for training and employment are available.

However, certain factors must be mentioned here. There still remains some resistance by men in the trades to women competing with them for the skilled and better paying jobs. A woman breaking into the machine trades must be prepared to face a certain amount of male hostility. However, by proving themselves equal in ability and by tactful behavior, women can overcome this problem, as has been proven in many cases. Another factor is the matter of pay. Despite the Equal Pay Law mentioned, some tendency persists to pay women

More and more women are entering the machining trades, and opportunities for training and employment are available. Photo: Ex-Cell-O Corporation.

less than men although both may be doing similar work. But this too is being overcome by women who are alert to the provisions of the law and who apply to the federal and local commissions set up to enforce it.

SUMMARY

The skilled metalworking trades offer, without a doubt, some of the most attractive career opportunities in industry or business. Many of the world's mechanical geniuses have been employed in the metalworking trades. Skilled workers in the tooling and machining industry are well paid. Employment security is unusually stable for highly skilled workers. Work conditions are generally pleasant, clean and safe. The average lifetime earnings for metalworkers rank among the highest of all skilled trades, and, in some instances, rival or exceed those in some professions. Opportunities for advancement are numerous. Toolmakers, moldmakers and machinists frequently rise to foreman or plant superintendent. Some go into engineering. Others become computer programmers. Many eventually open businesses of their own. Opportunities abound for the aggressive, motivated person who is willing to learn while he or she earns.

Above, assemblies for concrete pumping vehicles are being precision machined on a CNC-controlled horizontal machining center by a toolmaker. Below, a machinist prepares the final cut on a fixture using a large CNC jig bore. Photos: Remmele Engineering, Inc., St. Paul, Minnesota.

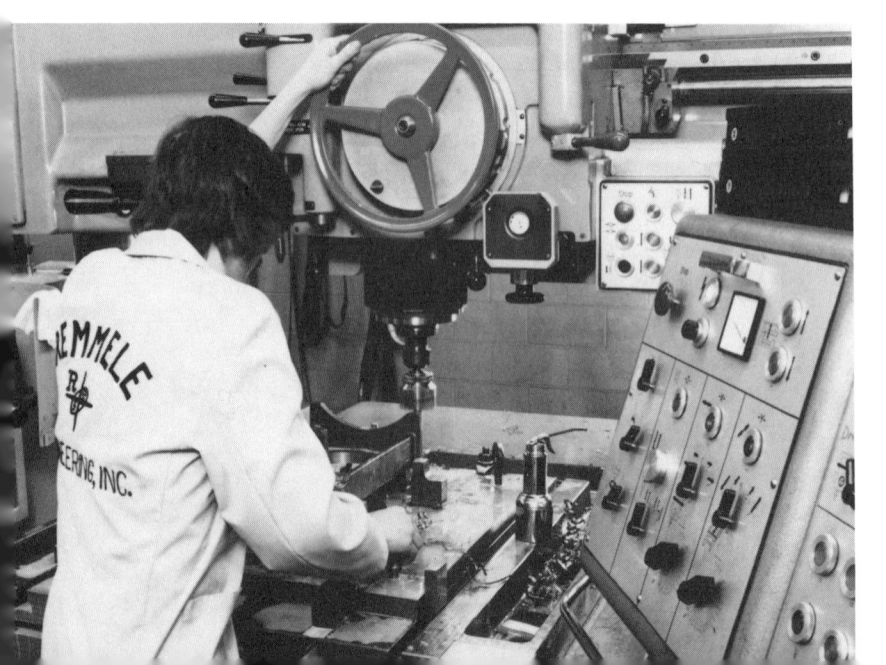

CHAPTER 2

MACHINE SHOP OPERATIONS

It has been estimated that there are over 350 different occupational specialties within the tooling and machining industry. Of course, not all of these jobs are classified as skilled. Therefore, only a few of the better-known, highly skilled jobs will be discussed in this chapter.

For further information regarding these job classifications and the host of others not discussed, consult the *Dictionary of Occupational Titles,* published by the U.S. Department of Labor, Bureau of Employment Security. That publication is available in the reference room of any good library. Most federal and state employment and labor offices also have a copy for reference purposes. Contact the State Department of Labor (consult your local telephone directory) or the Bureau of Apprenticeship and Training (BAT) office nearest you. A list of the main state offices and the regional BAT offices can be found in the appendix.

The *Dictionary of Occupational Titles* (DOT) reference numbers for the four most prominent occupational specialties discussed in this book are listed below:

Machinist	600.280-022
Moldmaker	601.280-030
Toolmaker	601.281-042
Tool and Diemaker	601.280-046

Generally, most workers enter skilled crafts after several years of intensive on-the-job training (OJT) combined with classroom instruction. Formal apprenticeship programs are the most common means of acquiring craft skills. Ways to enter the skilled metalworking trades will be discussed in Chapter 3.

The information in all the following job analyses is general. Jobs vary according to localities, products, and the particular conditions within the plants. Wage rates vary with locality and other conditions. For example, while most machinists are paid on an hourly basis, some workers, such as specialists in machine tool operation, can often earn more than their stated rates by using incentive plans or by doing piece work.

All wage information was extracted from an industry-wide survey conducted by the National Tooling and Machining Association in January 1985 in which 1,376 companies provided data on 26,993 employees.

Skilled metalworkers typically have opportunities for overtime work on a regular basis—the work week averages fifty hours. They have full-time work throughout the year as compared to some skilled workers who work only 50% to 80% of the year because of poor weather or poor economic conditions. For instance, in a special study of twenty-six skilled occupations conducted by the Bureau of Statistics of the U.S. Department of Labor, tool and diemakers ranked seventh in net lifetime earnings, close behind dentists, physicians and surgeons, several types of engineers, and owners and managers in finance, insurance and real estate.

MACHINIST ALL-AROUND

As the name implies, these highly skilled mechanics are capable of setting up and operating virtually all the standard machine tools of the machine shop. The machinist is capable of following a blueprint and finishing with a usable part. They can skillfully use all the bench and hand tools, harden and temper tool steels, sharpen the various tools and tool bits used in the shop, measure and cut metals within a thousandth of an inch or finer, use shop mathematics, read blueprints—in short they are at home in all the operations found in a machine shop. They can carry through from start to finish a wide variety of work without close supervision. In working, they consult blueprints and specifications or they may receive oral instructions.

All-around machinists plan the sequence of operations necessary to complete a job. This may require lathes, millers, shapers, drills, hand tools, and other apparatus. Knowing the properties of metals, they select and use them in accordance with needs. They may have to harden certain parts, grind them to close dimensions, and do filing, scraping, and fitting before the job is complete.

Many of these machinists are doing maintenance work in production plants where there is ample opportunity for exercising ingenuity in keeping the plant's production machinery and equipment in working order. Others become experimental machinists, working in laboratories, development and engineering plants, and the like.

The all-around machinist may become a toolmaker, diemaker, supervisor, master mechanic, or methods planner. Wages vary from $9.00 to $12.00 per hour, depending upon the locality and grade of machinist. The most skilled earn as much as $21.00 per hour. Machinists can find employment in almost any locality and any manufacturing industry.

All-around machinists should not be confused with machine operators who merely set-up and operate a specific single machine tool. These less skilled machine operators will do jobs which are more repetitive and production oriented.

TOOLMAKER

The mass production of metal goods depends largely upon the use of jigs, fixtures, gauges, and other tools. For example, to produce the bolt holes in the crankcase of an automobile engine, it is necessary to use a drill jig. It might be a box-like structure of cast iron into which the crankcase can be clamped. The drills are fed into the crankcase through drill bushings immovably fixed in the jig. Since each crankcase would be drilled like this, the distances between holes in all of them would be the same as the diameters of the holes. The jig must then be made with the utmost precision. Similarly, when the crankcase is machined on a mill, it is clamped in a fixture which ensures that all the cases are milled exactly alike. Similar principles govern other machining devices and tools used in manufacturing.

The toolmaker is an expert, all-around machinist who has specialized in making these production tools. Since these tools must be made to the utmost precision, the toolmaker becomes accustomed to working to dimensions which often must not vary to the half-thousandth of an inch or even finer. Consequently, the toolmaker must possess the highest degree of skill in the machine shop. He or she must be able to read and interpret the tool drawings or specifications, plan the procedures and operations that will produce the tool, make the necessary calculations, secure the tool steels and other necessary materials, operate any of the machine tools nec-

Diemaking demands accuracy and precision. Here, a supervisor and an apprentice discuss one of the die blocks from the lower die shoe of a very large progressive die. Photo: National Tooling and Machining Association.

essary to make the parts, harden and grind these parts, assemble, fit, adjust, and otherwise complete the tool, and do all of the other work entailed.

The work is interesting and varied and allows the toolmaker room for ingenuity and inventiveness. Promotion may be to tool designer, methods planner, or other supervisory positions. Wages vary from $10.00 to $12.00 per hour, depending upon experience, specialization, locality, and other considerations. Some of the most skilled might make over $25.00 per hour.

DIEMAKER

The diemaker is a toolmaker who has specialized in the making of punches and dies. These are high production tools which are set in presses to stamp out from sheet metal such products as the clip that holds the fountain pen in your pocket, the hooks and eyes used in dresses, or the metal body of your automobile. The dies are made to the finest of precision measurements and often cost large amounts of money.

What we have said of the toolmaker can be repeated in the case of the diemaker as each represents the highest degree of skill in the machine shop. Some diemakers become very specialized and make, for instance, watchcase dies or jewelry dies. They may earn as much as $25.00 per hour. The customary rates are $10.00 to $12.00 per hour.

TOOL AND DIEMAKER

The tool and diemaker analyzes specifications, lays out metal stock, sets up and operates machine tools and fits and assembles parts to make and repair metal working dies, cutting tools, jigs and fixtures, gauges and machinist hand tools, applying knowledge of tool and die designs and construction, shop mathematics, metal properties, and layouts and machining and assembly procedures, studies specifications, such as blueprints, sketches, models or descriptions and visualizes products. He or she computes dimensions and plans layout and assembly operations and sets up and operates machine tools such as lathe, milling machines, saws, and grinder to machine parts and verifies conformance of machine parts to specifications.

MOLDMAKER

Moldmakers are highly skilled machinists who specialize in building tools that shape plastic materials or soft metals while in a liquid state. Today it is nearly impossible to avoid everyday contact with plastic articles. The ballpoint pens we use, the steering wheels in our cars, the cabinets for our television and stereo sets, and our telephones are made of plastic and produced in quantity by precision molds. The widespread use of plastic products, which continues unabated, has created a shortage of skilled moldmakers which is growing more serious.

Moldmaking has been called an art as well as a skill. The moldmaker must possess the same skills and competencies previously described for diemakers and toolmakers. In addition, a moldmaker must have a strong working knowledge of plastics and a practical knowledge of thermodynamics. Plastics and other materials used in molds are heated to a workable temperature and compressed in a mold which may have a built-in heating and cooling system to regulate temperature.

INSTRUMENT MAKER

The instrument maker is a highly skilled, all-around machinist on the level of the toolmaker who works with inventors, scientists, and experimenters to develop their ideas and designs. Working from sketches, drawings, and verbal instructions, the instrument maker makes a model or prototype embodying these designs, often to very fine limits of measurements and shapes. The scientist, inventor, or experimenter uses this model to test ideas and then returns it to the instrument maker for correction, modification, and changes until either the final form is arrived at or the idea is discarded.

In addition to manual skills, therefore, the instrument maker must be well grounded in the basic sciences and mathematics and capable of working without supervision from sketches and other information. Wages vary from $9.00 to $12.00 per hour.

NUMERICAL CONTROL (NC) MACHINE OPERATOR

One of the most important recent developments in machining practices has been the successful automation of machine tools by a system known as numerical control. Using electronic circuitry and controls, it is now possible to program a series of machining operations, punch or otherwise prepare a tape, feed it through these controls, and cause a machine, such as a lathe, mill, or drill press, to automatically machine a part and duplicate this for as many pieces as required. All that needs to be done is to position this part and the machine will do the rest.

As a result, there has arisen a need for operators who can set up programs from blueprints, punch or otherwise prepare the tape, feed it into the controls, position the piece to be machined, set the machine in motion, make the necessary adjustments, oversee the operations, measure or otherwise check the results, and, in general, be responsible for the machine, the controls, and the production. Numerical control operators can be trained to specialize in just one system or machine, and need no particular skill as machinists, or they can add these specialized skills to their training background to make them more valuable to their employers.

Depending, therefore, on this aspect, the pay scales of numerical control machine operators may vary from $8.00 to $9.50 per hour. Some of the very best might make up to $15.00 per hour.

COMPUTER NUMERICAL CONTROL (CNC) MACHINE OPERATOR

The job of a CNC machine operator is very much like that of an NC machine operator. This person has to know everything the NC machine operator does as well as computers. The CNC machine tool has no paper or magnetic tape. It is controlled by commands transmitted by the computer which the CNC machine operator has entered through the computer keyboard. In some instances a large mainframe computer is used, but more commonly a smaller mini- or micro-computer is used.

ELECTRICAL DISCHARGE MACHINE (EDM) OPERATOR

This person is responsible for the set-up and operation of the electrical discharge machine. On a conventional EDM, the operator generally machines the electrodes used in the machining operation. A knowledge of basic physics, math and metallurgy is essential. The most recent development in electric discharge machining is the use of a wire rather than an electrode for ultraprecise cutting. A wire EDM operator must plot the path of the wire. Wages vary from $9.00 to $11.00 an hour. Some EDM operators make as much as $20.00 an hour.

ENGINE LATHE HAND OR OPERATOR

You might have seen a woodturning lathe. The engine lathe works on the same principle—the part to be finished is rotated or turned against it—except that it is a much more powerful and complicated machine than the simple speed lathe. It needs the power because it is used for turning all kinds of metallic parts into circular shapes. It is more complicated because the tools used for working on the metal can be adjusted to many angles and can be fed automatically into or across the work. In addition, many jobs other than straight turning can be done. These may be the cutting of all kinds of screw threads, taper and angular turning, boring holes, and other internal work. Engine lathes vary from small ones mounted on benches to the immense machines used for turning 16" gun barrels or ships' propeller shafts. All kinds of castings can be handled as well as the finest of precision jobs, such as boring the holes in jig plates and dies.

Engine lathe operators must be able to operate all standard types and sizes of lathes. They must first set up the machine, which means that they must be able to read and interpret the blueprint of the particular part they are to machine, mount the part in the lathe so that it is securely held, either on centers, on a faceplate, in a chuck, or in a collet, select and set the speed with which the lathe will turn the part to be machined, select the tool which will do the work, adjust and clamp it in the proper place and at the proper angle in the tool rest, and select and set the speed with which the tool will be fed longitudinally across the turning work, or into and across the work, or at an angle, whichever is needed. They then turn the work and shape it in accordance with the blueprint, measuring with the proper instruments, such as calipers, micrometers, and steel scales. They may also use indicators to true up holes and to perform similar tasks. In addition, they make special purpose set-ups for grinding, boring, and other operations.

Lathe operators should be able to grind tool bits or ends to the proper shape for turning whatever metal they are to be used on, such as the various kinds of steel, aluminum, cast iron, and bronze. They should be able to work to very fine measurements, often being held to dimensions which must not vary from specifications by more than one thousandth of an inch or perhaps even finer.

Engine lathe hands may be graded as first class—the top grade—second class, and third class. Graduates of vocational and technical high schools and adult trade courses and machinist apprentices may become lathe operators, which usually is an interesting and varied occupation. Wages vary from $8.00 to $10.00 per hour, depending upon the location of the job, the grade, and other considerations. An exceptionally skilled operator might make up to $20.00 per hour.

Lathe operators may become tool room or production specialists or may rise to become set-up persons, supervisors, and the like. The lathe operator has a good opportunity to become an all-around machinist, as this machine is the fundamental one in the shop.

MILLING MACHINE HAND OR OPERATOR

The milling machine differs from the lathe in that the work is held stationary on a table which moves past a rotating tool turned by a horizontal spindle, very much like a slicer where the food is clamped to a table which is moved past a rotating knife. Milling machines are of several types, such as the universal mill, in which the table can be adjusted to horizontal angles, and the vertical mill, in which the tool is rotated by a spindle held in a vertical instead of a horizontal plane. They are also made in various sizes from the bench type to the large production machines used in milling cylinder blocks in automobile plants.

The milling machine hand must be able to operate all the standard types and sizes of mills and should be able to set them up. This consists of reading and interpreting the blueprint of the part to be machined and figuring out the necessary sequence of milling operations to be performed; clamping the work to the mill table with clamps and T-bolts, by the use of a vise, by holding the part in an indexing head, or by any other feasible method, selecting the cutters necessary to the work, setting and clamping the cutters by using an arbor, a collet, or holder of any type, adjusting the table in relation to the cutters to get the desired machining results, selecting and setting the proper speed at which the cutters should rotate, selecting and setting the proper feed or speed at which the table and work will move horizontally or vertically past the cutter or across it, using proper measuring devices, such as indicators, height gauges, verniers, and micrometers, making the first cuts, and checking results.

The operations may be face milling, slab milling, form milling, straddle milling, or dovetail cutting. In addition, the operator should be able to make the necessary calculations and set the mill for such work as simple indexing (as in spline cutting), compound and differential indexing (for such work as cutting helixes), and jig boring, using the vertical mill with the various stops, graduated dials, indicators, and other devices.

The work is interesting and varied and often provides opportunities for the exercise of a great deal of ingenuity. There may be some heavy lifting, although mechanical lifting devices are usually provided. Graduates of vocational and technical high schools and trainees from adult courses may go in for this specialty, which may lead either to production or tool room work. Wages are from $7.50 to $9.50 per hour, varying with the locality, the grade of worker, and other considerations. Some milling machine operators have very specialized skills and command rates of over $18.00 per hour.

Promotion may be to set-up person or supervisor, or the specialist may go on to become an all-around machinist if he or she has the opportunity to learn the other machines.

DRILL PRESS HAND OR OPERATOR

Machines which are used for drilling holes are a familiar object even to those who have never been inside a machine shop. If you have ever done shop work in your school days, pursued some sort of hobby, or watched your car being repaired, you have probably used or seen a drill press. In the shop, these machines appear in a wide variety of types and sizes, such as the small sensitive drill mounted on a bench, the multiple spindle or gang drill, or the gigantic radial drill press used to drill holes in large castings or fittings.

Drill press work is largely repetitive. Once the job is set up, little skill is required to operate the machine. However, the drill press hand who can set up the machines must be able to clamp the work suitably on the drill press table or select the proper drill jig and select and set the necessary drills, reamers, counterbores, and countersinks as needed. He or she is then capable of choosing the correct speeds at which the drills are to rotate and the correct rate at which the drills are to feed into the work. The drill press hand must use the necessary measuring instruments, such as plug gauges, depth gauges, and micrometers, to check the work against the specifications. He or she must also set up for tapping or threading, using the right taps, tools, speeds, and feeds.

A machinist's helper may become a drill press operator. So may beginners who can be trained on the job. On the larger radial drills, however, where more skills are required, an apprentice may specialize in the work. Promotion may be to set-up person or supervisor. Wages vary from $6.50 to $8.00 per hour. Some highly specialized people who set-up and operate drill presses make over $18.00 an hour.

CYLINDRICAL GRINDING MACHINE HAND OR OPERATOR

The cylindrical grinding machine is similar to a lathe in that the work is rotated against a cutting tool. However, instead of the single point tool that is used in a lathe, the work is revolved against a grinding wheel which also rotates. Smooth surface finishes and closely held dimensions can be obtained with this machine, which is usually used for finishing work that has been rough-cut on a lathe. This type of grinder is made in many sizes and types, from the small machine found in tool rooms to the huge grinders used in finishing forgings, such as camshafts, crankshafts, and the like. There are many other specialized types of grinding machines. A person might become an expert on any one with adequate training and experience.

Grinder hands or operators should be able to operate and set up these machines. Working from blueprints and other specifications, they figure out the sequence of grinding operations needed for the particular part or parts. They then secure the part in the machine between centers, on a faceplate, in a chuck, or in any other device as needed and select the proper abrasive or grinding wheel needed to finish the part, depending upon its metallic composition and the kind of finish wanted.

Next, they choose the proper speeds needed for rotating the work and the grinding wheel. They also select the proper speed with which the work will feed past the grinding wheel or into it. After starting the machine and taking some cuts, the operators measure the result until they arrive at the dimensions called for, using such instruments as snap gauges, micrometers, and indicators. They perform such operations as grinding straight outside diameters, grinding to shoulders, and grinding angles and tapers. During the process, the grinding wheel wears away. In order to restore its shape and cutting qualities, the operators must dress the wheel with an attachment bearing a diamond cutting tool. As mentioned before, the operators usually hold dimensions to the thousandth of an inch and even finer.

The nature of the grinding operations may sometimes cause safety and health hazards. There may be considerable dust and there is always danger of wheels breaking while rotating. In addition, contact with the moving abrasive wheel may cause burns. These risks may be reduced by exhaust systems and safety guards.

Grinder hands are usually graduates of vocational and technical high schools or adult training courses, or they may be machinist apprentices from small shops where they may have received some training. They may advance to become set-up persons or supervisors. Wages vary from $9.00 to $11.00 per hour. Those unusually skilled grinding experts might make up to $20.00 per hour.

SCREW MACHINE HAND OR OPERATOR

The screw machine is an automatic or semiautomatic lathe which is used as a mass production tool. It operates on the principle of the lathe with a multitool turret which, once set up, can operate continually or automatically without further human aid until some change is required or more material is needed to be fed in. It is usually used for producing circular parts, such as screws of all types, which are machined from long metal rods or bar stock. The operator needs no special skills and can be trained quickly to watch a battery of such machines. We are concerned here, however, with the operator who learns how to set up the machine.

Setting up involves reading and interpreting blueprints of the part to be produced, figuring the sequences of operations, setting the bar stock in place for holding and feeding, selecting the tools for the job and arranging and clamping them on the turret and the machine, setting and adjusting the cams which control the automatic operation of the machine, selecting and setting the speed at which the machine is to revolve, and measuring the first finished part, making whatever adjustments are needed. The operator who, in addition to all this, can design, lay out, and cut the cams is considered top-grade. He or she should also be able to sharpen all the tools used.

The machinist apprentice may select this as a specialty. Graduates of technical and vocational high schools may also go into this line. A great deal of ingenuity and improvisation is required which may attract such people. Promotion may be to set-up person for a battery of machines, to a supervisory position, or to similar responsibilities. Average wages range from $8.00 to $10.00 per hour. Those possessing top skills might command as much as $20.00 per hour.

ASSEMBLER OR BENCH HAND

Machinery, instruments, tools, and other equipment are all usually composed of a number of parts fitted together or assembled. Each part has its assigned role and must fit properly into the whole affair. Except in mass production plants, a certain amount of handwork is necessary in the final assembly of a great deal of equipment as with dies, molds, special fixtures, machine tools, special production machinery, and so on. The assembler may scrape parts to fit, chip and file forgings and castings to suit, drill holes where necessary, adjust and align parts, bolt and otherwise fasten parts together, and perform other necessary fitting operations in accordance with blueprints and specifications. The assembler or bench hand becomes accustomed to working to close dimension tolerances using precision measuring instruments.

This is highly diversified and interesting work, often requiring a great deal of ingenuity and patience. It requires a good background, such as possessed by a graduate apprentice. An all-around machinist may specialize in this work. Promotion may be to supervisor. Wages range widely from $6.00 to $11.00 per hour depending upon the diversity of skills possessed.

INSPECTOR

A great deal of this country's success in the production of metal goods is the result of the extreme care exercised in checking or inspecting the finished work, including the individual pieces, the subassemblies, and the final assembled product. Inspection includes checking all measurements, dimensions, shapes, the quality of surface finishes, the operation of the parts, the assembly, and all the other items as required by blueprints and specifications. Quality control is critical.

An inspector must be able to figure out and set up all the necessary mechanical, electrical, hydraulic, and other apparatus needed for the above checkups. In addition, he or she may be responsible for inspecting work that is progressing through the shop, having the authority to accept or reject unfinished work still in process of machining or finished and ready for use. The inspector may inspect single pieces, small lots, or large numbers of similar parts. In addition, he or she may check measuring instruments, such as micrometers, verniers, snap gauges, other gauges of all sorts, and production tools, such as drill jigs, fixtures, cutting tools, and dies.

To accomplish all this, the inspector must have a good background of mechanical training and experience and a thorough knowledge of shop mathematics, blueprint reading, and related sciences. Super-sensitive inspection devices, using laser beams and electrical impulses, for example, have brought inspection departments to the front edge of technology.

In the last few years a relatively new profession, quality control, has sprung up in which inspection methods have been developed into a scientific approach to the whole problem of checking, thereby controlling the results of production. The top-grade inspector with a good mathematical background and some engineering education can find a future as a quality controller.

All in all, inspection is a highly skilled and diversified type of work. Of course, there are many branches. The production inspector who checks work in process need not be as highly skilled as the tool inspector.

Ordinarily, the best inspectors are recruited from among all-around machinists, toolmakers, and top machine operators. Promotion may be to chief inspector, shop supervisor, methods planner, or jobs of a like nature. Wages may vary from $8.00 to $10.00 per hour.

LAYOUT PERSON

When large castings or metal parts come into the shop for machining, they are usually set up on a flat, horizontal metal plate and marked to show where the

Precision in a tool, often to a thousandth of an inch, is of critical importance. Inspectors are therefore employed to guarantee quality. Above, an inspector measures small parts to insure accuracy before they are shipped to a customer. Below, an inspector compares the greatly magnified shape of a part to a template fastened to an optical comparator. With this precision inspection, machine sizes can be checked to a few thousandths of an inch and angles to less than a degree. Photos: Kenlee Precision Corporation, Baltimore, Maryland.

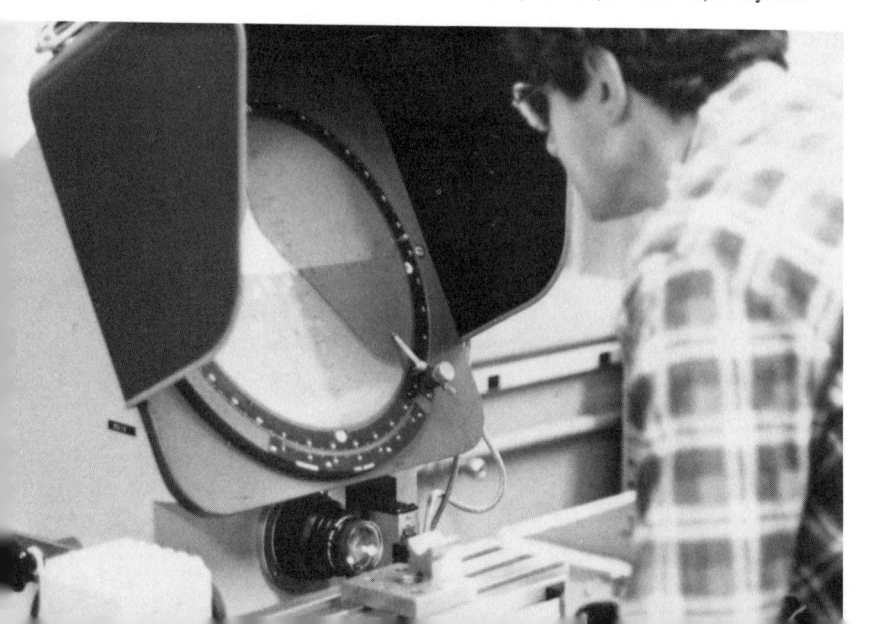

machining is to take place. This serves two purposes—it guides the machinists and it indicates whether or not enough metal has been allowed for all machine finishes. This work is called layout, and the person who does it is usually a specialized all-around machinist.

In working, he or she utilizes all sorts of marking and measuring tools to mark the guidelines, reference points, hole centers, and other important information on the castings and metal parts. The person responsible for layout must have a thorough knowledge of shop practice. He or she must know how the operators of the milling machines, boring machines, and others to whom the casting or part may go for machining will go about their work. The layout machinist must also be able to read and follow all sorts of blueprints and specifications and should have a knowledge of shop mathematics.

It takes from six to ten years of experience to develop the necessary skill for layout work. A person in this specialty may become a chief inspector or a supervisor, or may go into production planning. Wages may vary from $7.00 to $10.00 per hour.

THE FUTURE OF THE MACHINE SHOP

Mention has already been made of rapid technological advances in machine shop practices, such as laser beams, electronics, hydraulics, and compressed air and electricity to control and automate mass production and inspection of articles, as in automobile factories, for instance. Let's pause now to consider the future impact of such practices and the future role of the machinist.

The use of computerized numerical control (CNC) equipment for automating the machining of identical parts has already been mentioned. The use of computers is steadily increasing and is now a standardized part of shop practice. These types of developments have opened new opportunities for machinists to become programmers. These are but a few, and there will be many other opportunities and challenges for skilled machinists and operators.

Articles are appearing more frequently in technical journals and the daily press about the increasing use of robots in mass production lines, such as in automobile factories. These electronically or otherwise controlled devices perform an automatic operation repeatedly.

More and more of these automated devices and machines will be used in the future, but they will not replace the skilled machinist. Skilled machinists will be needed to build and maintain these systems.

However, some assembly-line people who used to do the tiresome, repetitive jobs which bored and discouraged workers will be displaced. Automated equipment and machines will eliminate many unskilled and semiskilled workers but they will also create new opportunities for the skilled worker.

Some predict that completely automated factories will produce articles without any personnel except a few floor monitors and inspectors. However, conversion to such sophisticated operations will be expensive. Furthermore, not all manufacturing processes can be so completely automated. Remember, these automated machines must be built and maintained by skilled people—machinists.

In short, while new technology will surely bring many more changes in manufacturing processes, the skilled person will always be needed. Skilled toolmakers, diemakers, moldmakers, and machinists are often called the high priests of mass production technology. They will continue to be at the leading edge of new production developments. Tremendous opportunities abound in the skilled metalworking trades for those aggressive individuals who are willing to learn new techniques and skills.

Remmele Engineering, Inc. runs a 6000 square foot training center with classroom facilities and a machine shop equipped with mills, lathes, saws, and other equipment. Up to 20 apprentices spend a year working under the watchful eyes of instructors. Photo: Remmele Engineering, Inc., St. Paul, Minnesota, and the National Tooling and Machining Association.

CHAPTER 3

HOW TO BECOME A MACHINIST

In every culture, people have transmitted skills from one generation to another. Most often the father and mother have passed their skills along to their children. Four thousand years ago, the Babylonian *Code of Hammurabi* made provisions for artisans to teach their crafts to youth. Later, the records of Egypt, Greece and Rome reveal that skills were still being passed on in this fashion.

During the Middle Ages the guild system evolved in Europe. This system of indenturing people for the purpose of teaching them craft skills was the forerunner of the apprenticeship system practiced today. When America was settled, craft workers coming to the New World brought with them the remnants of the guild system which has gradually evolved into today's apprenticeship system.

As an example, the American colonial patriot, Paul Revere, was a member of a family which was famous for its silversmithing. Paul and his younger brother, Thomas, had learned their craft from their father. In turn, two of Paul's sons served apprenticeships in the family's Boston shop. Paul himself later became a coppersmith and founded the American copper and brass industry in 1802, at the age of 67. His company later became part of the present-day Revere Copper and Brass Company which produces widely used cookware.

Another famous American, a contemporary of Paul Revere, was Benjamin Franklin. He, too, became an apprentice at twelve. Franklin was apprenticed to his older brother, James, to learn the art of printing. He later became famous as a printer and newspaper publisher, even before his other outstanding achievements and inventions.

The American apprenticeship system has grown and expanded considerably. Like America, it is still growing and changing. Today it serves a far different nation than the one of pioneer days. The new apprenticeship system now responds to scientific discoveries, new teaching methods, expanding industry, and an increasing population.

Apprenticeship has been, and continues to be, the most common method of entering the skilled trades. However, there are several alternatives. First, let's examine today's apprenticeship system.

WHAT IS APPRENTICESHIP?

Apprenticeship is a voluntary system of training in occupations that require a diverse range of skills and knowledge, as well as maturity and independence of judgment. It involves planned, day-by-day training on the job and experience under proper supervision, combined with technical studies in subjects related to the occupation.

Apprenticeship gives men and women comprehensive instruction and experience, both on and off the job, in all the practical and theoretical aspects of the work required in a skilled occupation. Through rotation from one division of work to another and related technical instruction, apprentices acquire additional skills, master the application of those already learned, and develop independence of judgment. This system enables them to be productive during their entire period of training.

Most apprenticeship programs in the metalworking trades are one to five years long. To master a particular trade, an apprentice must learn and perfect each skill and bring those skills up to the speed and accuracy required for the job.

APPRENTICESHIP LEGISLATION

The first legislation in the United States to promote an organized system of apprenticeship was enacted in Wisconsin in 1911. That law placed all apprenticeship activities under the jurisdiction of an industrial commission.

During the 1920s, many employers, labor organizations, educators, and government officials combined their efforts to bring about a national uniform apprenticeship system. The vital need for a comprehensive training system had become apparent during World War I and in the economic boom that followed.

In August, 1934, President Franklin D. Roosevelt created the Federal Committee on Apprentice Training as an advisory committee for the Secretary of Labor. That committee, today known as the Federal Committee on Apprenticeship, continues to advise the Secretary of Labor on all matters pertaining to apprenticeship training and education.

In 1937, the National Apprenticeship Act was passed by Congress. It created the Bureau of Apprenticeship and Training (BAT) under the U.S. Department of Labor to promote and supervise apprenticeship activities throughout the country. Many states have since enacted separate state legislation setting standards and requirements for apprenticeship programs. A list of the Federal Bureau of Apprenticeship and Training offices is contained in Appendix C. Correspondingly, a list of offices of those states which have separate apprenticeship agencies is in Appendix D.

THE VALUE OF AN APPRENTICESHIP

For young people just starting out in the world of work, apprenticeship has some very significant advantages. It provides an efficient way to learn skills because the training is planned and organized.

Apprentices earn as they learn because they are already working for a company. When their apprenticeship is completed, they are assured a secure future and a high standard of living because craft skills are in great demand by employers. The person who has completed an apprenticeship program is recognized as a skilled craft worker. Many employment and advancement opportunities which would not otherwise be open become available for the aggressive person who wants to move up.

Industry, too, benefits greatly from the apprenticeship system. Graduates are well-rounded craft workers, competent in all branches of their trade, and able to perform work without close supervision. Their intensive apprenticeship training enables them to use their imagination, ability and knowledge in their work. If changes are necessary in the production process, these craft workers provide the versatility needed for quick adaptation. Their skills are vital to industrial progress.

APPRENTICESHIP PROGRAMS

Apprenticeship programs are conducted or sponsored by employers. The employer identifies and defines the skills which are expected of a journeyworker. Typically, this identification and definition of skills is called the Apprenticeship Standard. A sample of the apprenticeship standards for a machinist program is shown later in this chapter.

The typical apprenticeship program has two major components:

1. On-the-job-training
2. Classroom instruction related to on-the-job training.

In the metalworking industry, an apprenticeship program is typically four years of on-the-job training encompassing approximately eight thousand hours (two thousand hours per year). While the apprentice is working on the job he or she will normally take at least 144 hours of classroom instruction per year. Most often this means two hours of class per night, twice a week during a 36-week school year, although this formula varies. A sample of the classroom component of an apprenticeship program for machinists also follows later in this chapter.

The employer and the apprentice employee enter into a formal written agreement which sets out the work processes which the apprentice will learn, the hours which will be worked, and the wages which the apprentice will be paid during the program. The employer agrees to provide employment and training and the employee apprentice agrees to learn the skills identified.

At the end of the apprenticeship program, the graduating journeyperson receives a certificate of completion, similar to the diploma awarded by academic institutions. An apprenticeship program is comparable, in many aspects, to an advanced academic program except that the apprentice is working and earning while learning. The certificates are issued either by the Federal Bureau of Apprenticeship and Training or the state apprenticeship agency.

The apprenticeship program is typically supervised by an apprenticeship committee composed of representatives of management and labor. Frequently, national trade associations and labor unions develop and provide much of the materials and content of the apprenticeship programs.

Every apprenticeship program has basic standards or rules which must be followed closely. Below are the essential ones:

- The starting age of an apprentice is not less than 16.
- There is a full and fair opportunity to apply for apprenticeship.
- There is a schedule of work processes in which an apprentice is to receive training and experience on the job.

- The program includes organized instruction designed to provide apprentices with knowledge in technical subjects related to their trade.
- The apprentice's progress, both in job performance and related instruction, is evaluated periodically and appropriate records are maintained.
- There is a schedule of wages with progressive increases for successful achievers.
- Proper supervision of on-the-job training with adequate facilities to train apprentices is insured.
- There is employee-employer cooperation.
- Successful completions are recognized.
- There is no discrimination in any phase of selection, employment or training.

In the metalworking trades, a machinist apprentice program includes an opportunity to become familiar with all major equipment used in the shop. In usually four years a novice or beginner can become a journeyperson machinist.

The apprentice is taught by competent shop people. Training generally begins with simple tasks and progresses to more difficult ones. The apprentice learns by actual practice how to set up and operate the standard machine tools. The apprentice also learns to use all of the bench and hand tools as well as all measuring and inspection instruments. The apprentice is taught how to read and interpret blueprints and apply practical shop mathematics to solve problems in shop procedure.

During this hands-on shop training the apprentice is also attending classes to learn the theory related to the various skills and processes which must be mastered during the apprenticeship program. Let's take a look at a sample on-the-job training (OJT) schedule and a sample classroom schedule for a machinist apprentice.

MACHINIST APPRENTICE PROGRAM
ON-THE-JOB TRAINING SCHEDULE

Process/Activity	*Hours*
TOOL CRIB	250
• Learn the names and types of all tools used in the trade	
DRILL PRESS	700

- Safety
- Lubrication
- Feeds
- Speeds
- Drill grinding
- Drilling
- Reaming
- Counterboring
- Lapping
- Tapping

MILLING MACHINE — 1,000

- Safety
- Lubrication
- Feeds
- Speeds
- General set-up
- Slotting
- Angle milling
- Dividing head
- Drilling
- Reaming
- Tapping
- Form milling

- Face milling
- Vertical milling
- Horizontal milling
- Boring
- Slab milling
- End milling

LATHES (Engine and Bench) — 1,000

- Safety
- Lubrication
- Feeds
- Speeds
- Reaming
- Face plates
- Set-up
- Facing
- Boring
- Tapping
- Drilling
- Threading
- Topper turning
- Straight turning

GRINDERS — 850

- Safety
- Lubrication
- Feeds
- Speeds
- Selection of grinding wheels
- Mounting wheels
- Taper grinding
- Form and angle grinding
- Jig grinding

NC and CNC — 450

- Safety
- Language
- Write and run program
- Selected tooling
- General set-up
- Control of machining

COORDINATE MEASURING MACHINE (CMM) — 50

- Safety
- Calibration
- Selection of inspection probe
- Checking dimensions
- Fixturing of workpieces
- Program CMM

How to Become a Machinist 69

ELECTRIC DISCHARGE MACHINE (EDM) 200

- Safety
- Select and shape electrode material
- Set-up workpieces

FILING MACHINE 200

- Safety
- Selection of machine files
- Straight and taper filing

CONTOUR CUTTING 200

- Safety
- Feeds
- Speeds
- Selection of saws
- Internal and external cutting

HEAT TREATING 400

- Safety
- Types of tool steels
- Treatment of tool steels
- Hardening and draw temperatures
- Carbide brazing
- Case hardening
- Annealing
- Hardness testing

BENCHWORK AND ASSEMBLY 2,400

- Safety
- Hand filing
- Layout work
- Assembling and finishing tools
- Hand tools
- Inspection tools

MISCELLANEOUS MACHINES 300

- Machinery repair
- Specialty work to attain the skills, knowledge and versatility required of journeypersons

TOTAL HOURS 8,000

MACHINIST APPRENTICE PROGRAM CLASSROOM SCHEDULE

Topic	*Classroom Hours*
FIRST AID	
• Treatment	8
BLUEPRINT	
• Lines	4
• Multiple view drawings	2
• Auxiliary/sectional views	4
• Dimensioning	14
• Shop sketching	8
• Shop layout	6
• Geometric dimensioning and tolerancing	36
• Surface texture symbols	8
MATH	
• General math	6
• Algebra	6
• Geometry	12

- Trigonometry 40
- Feeds and speeds 6
- Indexing head 6

BENCHWORK

- Measuring tools 14
- Noncutting tools 2
- Cutting tools 2

SHOP THEORY

- Safety 4
- Cutting fluids 2
- Saws 2
- Drill press 6
- Milling machine 40
- Engine lathe 58
- Grinder 62
- NC and CNC 54
- Electrical discharge machine 20
- Metallurgy 36
- Sawing 10
- CAD and CAM 30
- Tool steels 24
- Grinding theory 28
- Jigs and fixtures 32
- Turret Lathes 10
- Innovative technology 16
- Machinery's Handbook 22

TOTAL 640

HOW DO YOU GET STARTED?

If your school days are behind you and you have no particular metalworking skills, you will have to canvass and explore the industrial job market. If you are interested in becoming a machinist, what path can you follow?

One way is to pick up the trade, that is, get any kind of job in a machine shop which would bring you in contact with machines and tools. You might be an errand runner or a helper. By keeping your eyes and ears open and by taking every possible opportunity of practicing on the bench and on the machines, eventually you will learn enough to operate a machine or do some of the minor jobs around the shop. You might have to go from shop to shop to avoid repetitive work or getting into a blind-alley occupation.

Obviously this is an unstructured and haphazard way of learning the trade. It takes a great deal of time and it is unsupervised, discouraging, unsystematic, and apt to leave you with some bad trade habits or in some narrowly specialized job with no future. The best approach is the four-year formal apprenticeship method which provides specific, systematic, and logically progressive training in all the fundamentals of the trade under the skilled supervision of master machinists and teachers.

Most companies wish that the apprentice applicants be graduates of a high school, technical school, or vocational high school. Some employers even require that

Fourth-year apprentices are instructed in the use of a CNC (Computer Numerically Controlled) machine in their work. Computers play a more active role in machining today than ever before. Photo: Central Westmoreland Area Vocational-Technical School, New Stanton, Pennsylvania and the National Tooling and Machining Association.

the applicant be in the upper half of his or her graduating class. Most employers have a probationary period of six months during which the new apprentice must show promise or be dropped. Another consideration is the length of the training period.

Although the usual term of apprenticeship is four years or, sometimes, five years, this can be shortened under certain conditions.

Some time may be credited toward the apprentice program if the apprentice has graduated from a vocational or technical high school or for previous work experience in machine shops, or perhaps for machinist work performed as a member of the Armed Services.

There are also some excellent training opportunities besides apprenticeship programs. Many companies have highly structured training programs. Some include classroom instruction while some are strictly on-the-job training. Some programs are designed to produce machine operators or specialists rather than all-around machinists. The shop and the trainee *do not* enter into a contract or agreement. The trainee is hired and taught to use a machine, such as an engine lathe or drill press, by one of the experienced operators. The trainee generally starts with simple jobs and progresses to the more difficult ones until the work can be performed without supervision. The training period may vary from six months to a year or more, depending upon the type of work the particular shop produces. The graduate of this type of program may become a semiskilled production machine specialist or advance to a skilled tool room machine operator. The graduate may also learn to read blueprints and do shop mathematics.

This is one way to make a start in the machinist trades without going through a long apprenticeship. With proper supervision, motivation, and hard work, the path may lead to all-around skills opportunities.

However, suppose you cannot secure an apprenticeship or training opportunity such as described. What then? If you are still determined to be a machinist, you can explore the courses given by public, private, and semipublic agencies.

Many cities and communities operate skills centers where adults may secure either free or for a small fee the basic training they need to enter a trade. These skills centers are supported by state or federal government funding. Check with the nearest employment service office.

In many cities there are good public and private trade and technical schools. However, you should make careful inquiry before signing up at any private institutions. Be wary of schools that claim to turn out highly skilled mechanics in a short period of time. Make sure their claims of immediate job placements are valid. Do not be pressured into signing any contracts. Be careful, too, to check out the course content of the public vocational technical schools because, even though the training may be free or nominal in cost, if the program does not teach useful skills, it will be a waste of your time.

Although the great majority of private vocational schools do a good job of instruction and placement and have good records of reliability, make careful inquiry before signing up for training.

In New York, for example, the State Consumer Protection Board found that some private schools were enrolling trainees who were patently unqualified. Some trained people for occupations in which there were few openings for beginners. Others took advantage of low-income applicants who were eligible for government tuition grants. Because of such abuses, some state and local governments have strengthened regulations on these schools. However, not all abusive practices have been eliminated—be careful!

The following suggestions might help you to select a proper school:

- Watch out for the blind advertisement. Make sure the name and address of the school are given in the ad. Try to verify any advertising or other claims that sound exaggerated. Think twice about schools that, "guarantee employment," but expect placement service to be offered. Beware of "high-pressure" sales talks. Check out the school with your local Better Business Bureau.
- Check the view of prospective employers in your area. What do they think of the recent graduates of the school?

- Look for well-defined admissions requirements, an in-depth interview and/or some type of standardized admission test. Be sure you understand your ranking or grade on the test.
- Visit the school personally and talk with the instructors. Have they had practical experience in data processing?
- Ask the school for names and addresses of graduates in your own locality. Ask these graduates for their opinions of the school's courses, faculty, and services.
- Be sure you get a receipt for your tuition down payment and a copy of the enrollment agreement.

Many of the suggestions above were gathered from accrediting criteria set by the Accounting Commission for Business Schools and the National Association of Trade and Technical Schools.

To get impartial information and descriptive printed materials, write to: National Home Study Council, 1601-18th Street, Washington, D.C. 20009, and to the National Council of Technical Schools, 1507 M Street N.W., Washington, D.C. 20005.

In addition, you can get advice from your local office of the Veterans Administration, the regional office of the Federal-State Employment Service, the Local YMCA counseling service, and the vocational guidance services of local colleges and schools. The state apprenticeship agencies and Bureau of Apprenticeship Offices of the U.S. Department of Labor, should also be contacted for further apprenticeship information. Several national and local trade associations and labor unions can provide assistance, advice and literature. Lists are provided in the Appendix.

FEDERAL AND STATE TRAINING ASSISTANCE

In 1962, the Manpower Development and Training Act was enacted by Congress. This legislation funded a broad program of training and retraining of unemployed and underemployed workers in various trades and occupations where jobs were available. The Act enabled thousands of people to improve their basic education and make a start in some skilled occupation. The Comprehensive Employment Training Act was enacted in 1974. It absorbed and expanded the federal training programs being conducted under the Manpower Training Act.

In 1982, the Job Training Partnership Act (JTPA) was passed to replace the Comprehensive Employment and Training Act. This new act marshalls federal, state and local government resources to help economically disadvantaged and long-term unemployed people gain skills.

For the metalworking industry, the National Tooling and Machining Association (NTMA) has conducted a special full-time pre-employment training program for people interested in metalworking careers. NTMA, with federal funding assistance since 1964, and now under JTPA, has provided valuable pre-employment training to more than 17,000 persons. That program is an accelerated, 12-week course including hands-on training, on the milling machines, lathes, grinders, saws and drill presses, and classroom instructions in basic shop math, blueprint reading, machine shop theory, and benchwork skills.

This special pre-employment training program conducted by NTMA is the largest continuous nationwide program of its type. Many of the innovative procedures and practices developed in this program have been adopted by other organizations. These federal training programs have helped thousands of people secure basic education and training to enter the active workforce of America. If you are eligible, contact your local government employment service office to see if any JTPA programs are currently being offered in your community.

Several states also fund training and educational programs. Consult your local government employment service office for information on programs in your community.

VETERANS TRAINING PROGRAMS

For eligible veterans, apprenticeship offers special opportunities. When a veteran enters an approved apprenticeship program, he or she may receive—in addition to wages—a monthly training assistance allowance under the Veteran's Pension and Readjustment Assistance Act of 1967.

As a result of their military training, some veterans will already be eligible for craftworker status when they are discharged. The U.S. Department of Labor recognizes and has certified many of the military occupational specialties so military work experience can often be credited toward a civilian craft program.

If you are a veteran, you should inquire at any Veterans' Administration office or the nearest government employment service office. The local posts of the American Legion, or the Veterans of Foreign Wars can also provide advice and assistance.

IF YOU ARE UNDER 18 YEARS OLD

If you are about to enter high school or are already in high school and are interested in a metalworking career, enroll in a machine shop or machine trades course if it is offered at your school. Many high schools have excellent vocational technical programs.

If your school offers such a program, typically half of your school time will be spend studying the usual English, social studies and other academic courses. The other half of your program will be devoted to special classes where you will learn shop mathematics, science and blueprint drawing. You will also receive substantial hands-on practice in the school machine shop. After graduation you will have a big head start on people who have not been so fortunate. However, do not expect to be treated as a first class machinist when you graduate. You will still have more training and classroom study before you reach that status.

A technical school course differs from a vocational course because it provides less shop work and puts greater emphasis on sciences and mathematics. Also, the technical courses are arranged to allow sufficient credits for entrance to a college engineering or science program. The technical course will usually provide a sufficient number of machine shop and related courses to give you a good start in industry.

If you are already in high school and committed to a college entrance curriculum, it may be too late for you to change, even though you might now want to become a machinist. In that case, it is best for you to finish your studies and get your diploma. Concentrate on mathematics and science and, if possible, take mechanical drawing and all the general metal shop work you can. Many metalworking firms will offer apprenticeships to high school graduates who can demonstrate a sincere desire and have good grades in high school math, science and mechanical drawing.

An apprentice uses a belt sander to remove burs from small parts workpieces. Credit: Kenlee Precision Corporation, Baltimore, Maryland.

STAY IN SCHOOL

If you are in high school and are thinking of dropping out to get a job—*don't!* Under present day conditions, the minimum acceptable educational background for any sort of job with a future is a high school diploma. There will be very little place at all for the uneducated and the unskilled in the future except in the most menial, dead-end jobs. As industrial and commercial life becomes more mechanized and automated, only the alert, the informed, and the skilled will be wanted. A high school diploma is a must as a guarantee that you have had at least a basic education. A high school diploma is required for all civil service jobs and for most apprentice programs.

A high school graduate will earn more income from age 18 to retirement than a person with only an elementary school diploma. Numerous studies conducted under varying economic conditions show that persons with more schooling earn more money. The cultural and social advantages that come with higher education may well be worth the time, money, and effort required to stay in school, even if the immediate economic advantages should cease to exist.

Get your high school diploma. Don't let the promise of an available job and the expectation of a weekly paycheck and money in your pocket lure you away. The job may end, and you could find yourself in the ranks of the unskilled and unwanted looking for almost any-

An apprentice cuts a shoulder on a shaft using an ID-OD Grinder (inside diameter - outside diameter). Photo: National Tooling and Machining Association.

thing to do. If, however, circumstances are such that you have no choice, then you should try to complete your high school requirements at night school or possibly through a good correspondence school. It is an absolute must!

PUZZLED ABOUT YOUR FUTURE?

Finally, suppose you are already at work in a metalworking plant in some narrowly specialized job such as operating a production machine or doing some routine bench work. The chances are that you cannot get any experience or practice which will enable you to become a machinist. You have found it most difficult to break away from this production work since you must keep your job, and perhaps you are worried about the future.

The way out is through evening and other trade extension courses which are offered by practically every large community in the country and by the large, reputable correspondence schools. Such cities as Chicago, Los Angeles, New York, and Philadelphia conduct evening classes in machine shop practice where you can learn to operate all the machine tools, use the precision measuring instruments and hand tools, and, in short, prepare yourself to break away from the ranks of the semiskilled. In addition, you can learn the necessary trade mathematics, blueprint reading and drawing, and related science through the same channels or by taking correspondence courses.

Of course, it is not easy. It means sacrificing your evenings. It will require hard study after a day's work, but it is worthwhile. Thousands of top-grade machinists have taken this road. Get in touch with your local board of education and vocational advisory services to find out about these courses.

ADDING IT ALL UP

What has been said in this chapter about becoming a machinist adds up to the following:

- If you are under 18 years of age and ready for high school, your best choice is a vocational high school; next would be a technical school. If you are in high school already and cannot make the change, it is best to finish and get a diploma.
- The best approach to learning the trade is through a systematic, organized apprenticeship in a good shop. This may be under the auspices of the local apprenticeship council or may be just a particular company's scheme. As long as it offers a bona fide, systematic, all-around approach to the trade, it is worth taking.

- If you cannot see your way to an apprenticeship then you may be able to find a shop which will put you on as a learner or beginner and make you a machine specialist within a year. This may be a start from which you can advance to higher skills.
- If you are over 18 and are already at work, you can use the local evening trade extension school or skills center. Or you can go to a good private trade school. Some correspondence schools also offer valuable material.
- Go to the nearest U.S. Employment Service Office and inquire about special trade training courses funded under the Jobs Training Partnership Act or a state-funded program.
- Stay in high school and earn your diploma.

An engineer uses a CAD (computer aided design) system to design and test machinery on a terminal. The right screen magnifies sections of the drawing from the left screen so that the engineer can inspect these sections more thoroughly. Photo: National Tooling and Machining Association.

CHAPTER 4

EMPLOYMENT AND ADVANCEMENT

There are many roads to finding a job as a machinist once you have acquired your basic training. These paths can vary with your personality, background, training, and particular situation. Let's now examine some possible approaches.

You have several alternatives if you are a graduate of a vocational or technical high school. You can try to secure an apprenticeship in a metalworking plant; successfully completing it will assure your future as an all-around machinist. We have indicated how this can be done in Chapters 2 and 3. However, you may not be able to do this or you may have no desire to go through a long and arduous learning period. In that case, you ought to first try to take advantage of the contacts your school and teachers probably have with local industry. Most vocational and technical high schools maintain a more or less formalized employment service for their students. Since they are training skilled help for industry, they must keep in contact with actual conditions in the field. In fact, most of these institutions have advisory boards composed of leaders from both management and labor who help to keep the schools' courses of study in line with the current needs of the occupations. In this way, your teachers and advisors are kept aware of employment needs and can help you in finding a job somewhere in the community where you can make a start in your trade.

Many of these schools, too, operate what are usually called cooperative or work-study courses. The usual procedure here is to find jobs in industry for the senior-term or last-year students who thus go to school and work alternate weeks. This method gives students practical, industrial, paid shop experience for one week and classwork in the related and academic subjects on alternate weeks. This pattern may vary in particular localities. If you have had the benefit of this experience, you have already made some industrial contacts and perhaps found a shop where you can get started full time when you graduate.

Suppose, however, you have graduated from a school which does not offer these opportunities and you cannot secure a job. There are several things you can then do. The first, of course, is to watch the want ads in the daily newspapers of your town and apply for those jobs which seem to fit your capabilities. If you are asked to write a letter of application to any of those ads, make sure your letter is standardized in form, properly addressed, legibly written or neatly typed, and contains the requested information. You might make up a standard form letter for yourself containing a brief introductory statement of your personal qualities, including such data as age, marital standing, and a chronological account of your education and special training, as well as a list of your experience and qualifications as a machinist. The last paragraph should state briefly why you think you could fill the job adequately. End the letter with the standard closing. Including a stamped, self-addressed envelope might be helpful.

At the same time, you should register with the local office of your state employment service. The various states, in cooperation with the federal government, operate 1,800 full-time local employment exchanges and more than 2,000 part-time offices throughout the United States. These agencies do much more than merely list job openings. They also offer an expert vocational guidance service of which you should take advantage to make the best possible use of your training and background. For veterans, preferential treatment is the rule. If you have some slight physical disability, you might also get special assistance. All in all, it would be decidedly to your advantage to make use of this efficient and free service.

There also are many reputable, private employment agencies which have good contacts with industry. It might help you to register with one of these. Of course, if you are placed in this way, you will be charged a fee which will vary in accordance with the local customs and laws.

These methods do not exhaust all the possible job approaches. For example, you can apply directly to the employment offices of all the machine shops in your vicinity. If you are really determined and have sufficient stamina, you might go through the telephone directory and list all the machine shops by neighborhood groups and then systematically call at each for a personal interview.

What has been said so far can apply in some degree to any of you, whether you have acquired your basic machine skills in a vocational high school or by any of the other methods indicated in Chapter 3. At the risk of some repetition, let's list the possible job approaches as follows:

- Consulting want ads in the newspapers.
- Answering want ads with a letter and résumé.
- Placing situation wanted ads in the newspapers.
- Using the employment services of the institution where you received your training.
- Making personal calls at all available shops.
- Using the services of the public and private employment agencies and offices.
- Using the business connections and acquaintances of friends and relatives.

- Using union hiring halls.
- Contacting trade associations and their local chapters.

During your training period, you should have become acquainted with and read whenever possible such excellent trade periodicals as *American Machinist, Machinery, Modern Machine Shop,* and others. Reading these journals gives not only an overall picture of modern shop practices but also an up-to-date report on business conditions throughout the country. Those articles will often pinpoint particular spots where better opportunities might exist. If you are willing to move, all this information will be valuable in getting started.

Let's consider one of the most important elements of a job search—the interview. After you have filled out the application in the employment office of a particular shop, having carefully and legibly answered every question to the best of your ability and knowledge, you are ready for the interview with the employment manager, the shop superintendent, or a department supervisor.

INTERVIEWS

Do not for a moment think that because the machine shop trades involve a certain amount of dirt and grime that you can apply for a job dirty and sloppily dressed. You can try it, but the odds of your getting a job will be against you, especially if you are a beginner. First impressions are very important, and the prospective employer may see in your careless, sloppy appearance a similar attitude toward your work. Good machinists take pride in keeping themselves and their surroundings as neat and clean as circumstances will allow.

Whether you are applying in person, over the phone, or by mail, you will want to put your best foot forward when applying for that *first job*. You will want to make the best possible impression on an employer. This means being prepared to present yourself and your qualifications effectively.

Fortunately, or unfortunately, first impressions during the interview *do* count. The employer will judge by what he or she sees.

This does not imply that you need wear your best suit in looking for a job. Just make sure the clothes you are wearing are clean and presentable. If you have long hair, be sure that it is clean, neat, and not too long for safety in a shop situation. Why handicap yourself? Watch your language and do not try to oversell yourself and your abilities. For example, do not try to give the impression that you are an all-around machinist if all you can do is run a lathe or milling machine.

Consider the following list of suggestions which was developed by the guidance department of a large vocational-technical high school in New York City for the use of its graduating classes.

- Be neat and well-groomed.
- Check to be sure that your clothes are clean and pressed.
- Have your shoes polished and in good condition.
- Have your hair and fingernails neat and clean.
- Watch your English at all times, avoiding current fads of pronunciation and slang.
- Let the employer see that you are truly interested in the job for which you are asking to be considered.
- Show some enthusiasm for the job and the company.
- Take aptitude tests and complete application forms willingly and cheerfully.
- Do not be too modest! Inform the employer of your special abilities, skills and interests.
- Do not be afraid to ask questions and respond politely and honestly to those asked of you.
- Do not be afraid to smile occasionally.
- Try to relax and be yourself.
- When the interview is over, thank the interviewer and walk out.

In many instances it is wise to follow up the first interview after the lapse of several days with another personal call. You must convince the employer that you are really interested in working for the company. *Be brief at this time* because your only purpose is to keep yourself in the company's memory.

If you apply by letter or telephone, remember that you need to impress the employer with your qualifications so that he or she will want to consider you further. Your telephone voice and manner or your neatly typed, well-worded letter will give a clear picture of you. Correct spelling is very important.

In the past, it was possible to get work after a direct interview with a shop supervisor or department head. On the basis of the information in your application blank and a few questions, you might be hired and told when to report. While this simple system is still followed by some employers, most companies today take a few more precautions when hiring because it is very costly to hire people quickly and then be forced to fire them for incompetence or other reasons. As a result, you may be asked to take some tests. For example, you may be required to read and answer questions about some shop blueprints; you may have to make some simple calculations based upon these prints. Many large firms administer certain standard mechanical aptitude tests to check whether or not you do have the dexterity or mechanical deftness you claim to possess. You may have taken some form of these examinations before, in school or with some vocational counseling service. Some companies have developed entire batteries of tests by which they can determine with a considerable degree of certainty whether or not you are worth hiring.

In addition to these technical aptitude examinations, you may be required to take a standard pencil and paper test which will evaluate you personally. It may surprise you to know that your prospective employer is just as interested in your behavior and attitudes toward other people as he or she is in your mechanical skills.

Many surveys have shown that more people lose their jobs for some personality difficulty than because they are incompetent in their work. You can see why the employer will try to avoid hiring the person who is always unhappy and disgruntled, who is always complaining, who is forever bickering with the other workers or the supervisors, or who, in short, is a potential troublemaker in the organization. To prevent this situation, many companies give all job applicants a social behavior test. They may use a standard form purchased from a psychological testing service or publisher, or they may develop their own. At any rate, you can expect to encounter this sort of testing in your search for a job.

The New York State Employment Service published a pamphlet entitled *Why Young People Fail to Get and Hold Jobs.* This two-part pamphlet contains twenty-four actual case histories showing how attitudes and behaviors of certain young people prevented them from landing their first jobs. It also contains seventeen actual experiences of other beginning workers whose attitudes and behaviors cost them their jobs. Write to the Department of Labor, Employment Service, Albany, New York, for a copy. It's well worth the trouble.

Here are a few suggestions made in the pamphlet:

- Your appearance can be the difference between getting the job and getting the brush-off.
- Attitude and behavior play almost as important a part in getting and holding a job as does skill.
- Ignorance of labor market facts can result in costly mistakes.
- Misrepresentation is bound to be discovered and work to your disadvantage.
- Sensitivity about a physical defect can be a serious obstacle to getting and holding a job, if you let it.
- Unrealistic wage demands greatly increase the odds you won't get the job.
- Absence or lateness without good reason can cost you your job and could make it difficult to get another one.
- Insufficient training is an obstacle to getting the job you want.
- Insistence in doing the job your way most likely will create animosity and work to your disadvantage.
- Balk at entry requirements and you are likely to miss your big opportunity.
- Apply for a job with a friend along and you probably won't be hired.

CIVIL SERVICE

When you are canvassing the field for a start as a machinist, do not overlook the possibilities presented by the civil service whether it be federal, state, county, or city. This idea may surprise you. Many people think of civil service as a white-collar occupation, but it takes workers of many diverse trades to help operate and maintain our various governments. For instance, the federal government builds and services warships at Navy yards where, under civil service, such trades personnel as welders, shipwrights, machinists, and electricians are employed. Big cities, such as New York, Chicago, Boston, and Philadelphia, operate and maintain great transit systems, bridges, parks, fleets of trucks, and shops which require the services of numerous mechanics, all under civil service.

Entrance into a civil service job is by competitive examination. As a beginning machinist you would probably have to file for the helper or apprentice category. You would probably be required to take a written technical test on the fundamentals of the machine shop trades and a performance test on which you would have to do some machine operations on a part, working from a blueprint. A thorough physical examination is also usually given. Successful applicants are placed on a list in accordance with their marks and, as a rule, are appointed as vacancies occur. Advancement in civil service depends on competitive examinations also, with seniority on the job counting high.

The one great disadvantage of civil service work is the danger of getting into a rut. It can be like a featherbed into which you sink and become so comfortable that

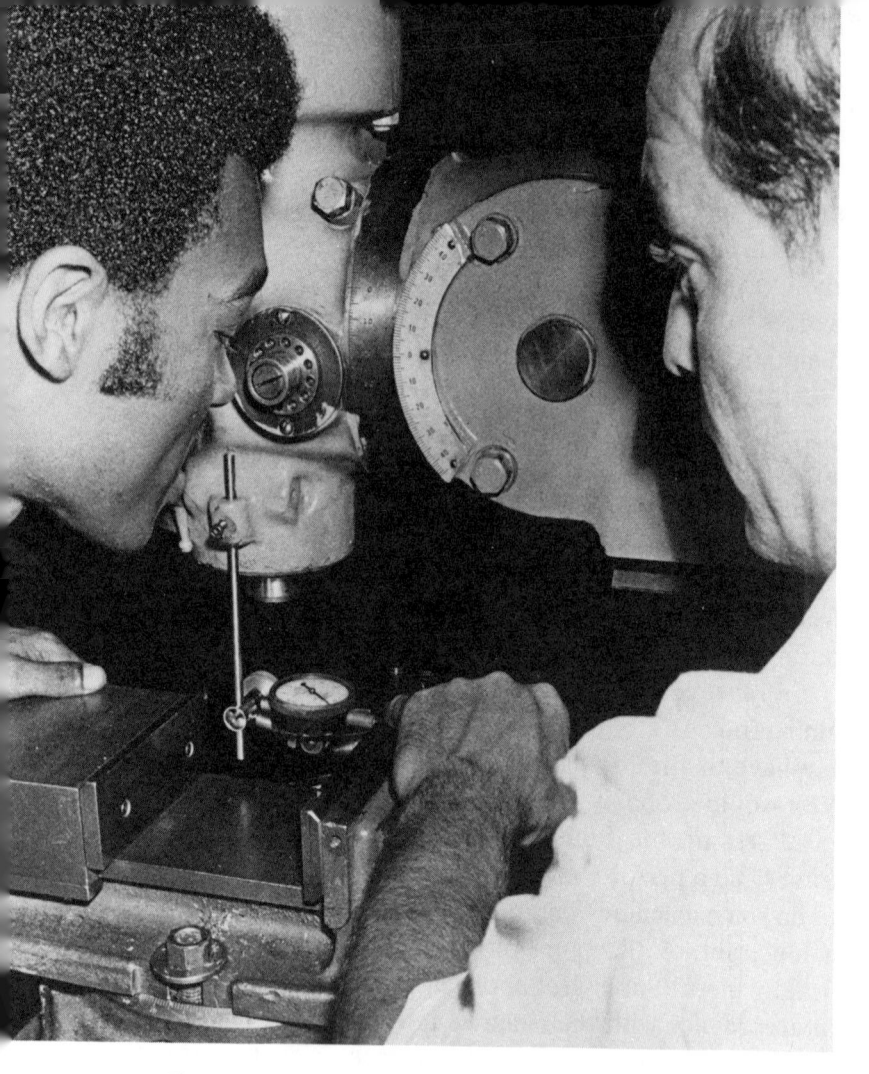

First-class, all-around machinists, toolmakers, and diemakers are developed only after years of studying and applying their skills. Here, an instructor shows a student how to align a milling machine head so it will be parallel to the vise jaws. While this is a simple operation, it must be done with absolute accuracy and precision to obtain the desired result. Photo: NTDPMA Detroit Training Center, and the National Tooling and Machining Association.

you may in time lose any initiative or desire for ventures on your own in private industry. However, an alert and ambitious person will not allow this to happen, and many persons have spent happy and useful lives serving the government.

To find out about government employment, inquire at your local civil service commission. You can also write to the United States Civil Service Commission, Washington, D.C., for a pamphlet titled *How to Get a Job with the U.S.A.* and other free information. Many large cities have newspapers or periodicals devoted entirely to civil service affairs. Get copies of such newspapers and follow them up. A career in civil service may be the answer for you. (A list of the regional offices of the U.S. Civil Service Commission can be found in Appendix B.)

ADVANCEMENT

It takes at least ten years of constant application to become a top-grade machinist. First-class, all-around machinists, toolmakers, and diemakers are produced only by lengthy experience. The factors that distinguish these topnotchers are their mechanical versatility and their ability to fashion metals to the utmost limits of accuracy and precision. Not only are they at home with every machine, tool, material, and process in the modern machine shop, but they are also able to use these with economy of effort to produce work that is often held to ten-millionths of an inch.

Measuring and holding work to the thousandth of an inch was commonplace long ago when the micrometer was invented. With the improvement of machine shop methods as time passed and the invention of the vernier and the extremely precise gauge blocks used today, it was possible to measure and work to a ten-thousandth of an inch. Further improvements in precision blocks, the development of the comparator, and the invention of electrical and optical methods of measuring have made it reasonable to demand even finer precision. Another example is the mirror-like surface finishes required on some parts. A surface finish of five tenths (0.5) of a microinch is often called for. A micro-inch is one millionth of an inch (0.000001 inch).

It is this painstaking care and accuracy that have made possible the success of our mass production methods. Our automobiles are assembled from thousands of parts which must go together at once and fit without handwork or delay as they flow on the assembly lines. Each separate part must, therefore, be made by the thousands and all exactly alike. Every camshaft and every fender that goes into a particular model of engine or car must be the exact duplicate of every other camshaft or every other fender of its type.

To make this possible, each step of manufacturing must be closely controlled. This is done by the use of specially designed automatic machines, dies, jigs, fixtures, and gauges. In addition, to ensure that all shapes and measurements are in accord with specifications, such measuring instruments as gauges, either mechanical or electrical, comparators, precision blocks, optical flats, surface plates, and sine bars are used.

If the product is to be held to these fine limits of accuracy, the tools and dies used for producing and measuring the pieces must be held to even finer limits. The degree to which this is accomplished determines the success of the final assembled product, whether it be an automobile, a machine tool, a pair of roller skates, a jet plane, a machine gun, or any other of the products that distinguish our machine age. Machinists such as tool and diemakers produce these tools, and it is readily understandable why it takes many years of experience to produce the topnotch tool.

At this point it may be worthwhile to emphasize that it is not only superlative manipulative skills that distinguish these mechanics. They are also highly skilled in the related technology of the machine shop. The most intricate and complex drawing or blueprint keeps no secrets from them. They are well versed in shop mathematics such as trigonometry and have a thorough understanding of the basic sciences underlying shop practices. They are also skilled in the heat treatment of metals. All this and more are necessary abilities for a topnotch tool and diemaker and are the reasons why, in the training of the aspiring machinist, the related technical subjects are all emphasized.

However, not all beginners are going to become tool and diemakers. Some must be content with other stations in the trade. All-around machinists, just short of the top bracket, are still highly skilled and versatile mechanics who have spent at least five or six years acquiring their skills. They may be employed at turning out intricate and accurate metal parts or some parts of lesser accuracy. If they have the drive and ambition, they might get an opportunity to become toolmakers.

Because of the specialized training and talents of toolmakers, there usually is a shortage of them. To compensate for this shortage, many large shops employ machine tool specialists to make the separate parts going into a jig, fixture, die, or tool. These parts are then assembled into complete units by specialized bench hands or assemblers. Many large production shops devote entire floors to particular types of machines. One may have scores of lathes of all types run by lathe operators; another may have similar banks of milling machines, turret lathes, grinding machines, or planers and shapers, all operated by specialists. The machinists operating all these machines are usually adept at one particular type and are capable of keeping up with production schedules. They may be producing the parts going into a machine tool or an automatic machine that manufactures cigarettes.

These specialized machine tool operators need four to five years of experience to be fully productive. Their narrow scope of work may prevent them from acquiring the necessary experience to reach the top all-around skills unless they can go from job to job, each time operating a different machine or perfecting a different shop technique. However, there are many who are content to be good lathe hands or milling machine operators, especially since these jobs pay well.

The big mass production manufacturing plants, such as the automobile plants, also employ machine operators, but these people are in a different category entirely. Usually they operate machines which are automatic in their cycle of work and, once set up, only require the operator to feed them and take out the finished pieces. Such workers need not be skilled machinists and can usually be trained within a short period of time.

The people who set up and check these machines for the operators, however, are usually skilled, even though they may be narrowly specialized. They may be operators who have spent some years with the machines and have acquired a thorough knowledge of them.

In the case of the automatic screw machines which turn out small cylindrical parts, they may be machinists who have specialized and learned how to make and set the necessary cams and adjust the cutting tools. Here too, this narrowing of experiences will work against this set-up machinist's reaching top skill status, unless he or she gets around from shop to shop and from machine to machine. Again, many are content with this step since it is an interesting job and often pays well.

We have mentioned that one of the fundamentals of mass production is the necessity for constantly checking shapes and sizes against specifications. This is done by inspectors who are well versed in the use of measuring instruments. Inspection may consist of running the parts through an automatic checking device or gauge in which case it is just a routine job and can be done by people with very little training. The inspector roams the shop and checks the products as they come from the machine. Since this requires training, some companies prefer machinists for this work. Again, it may mean using all the intricate measuring tools, such as verniers, comparators, precision blocks, sine bars, optical flats, and others. This type of inspection is usually done by a machinist who has had at least five years' experience as a mechanic or by a machinist apprentice who has decided to specialize as an inspector. In large plants, he or she may rise to chief inspector, a very responsible job. In recent years, this job of checking products has become a scientific operation known as quality control with a statistical approach; it offers attractive opportunities to mechanics with mathematical aptitude.

It may be helpful at this point to recapitulate. As a beginning machinist, you have before you numerous avenues to a good livelihood. If you have had a firm basic training and wish to become an all-around machinist and then a toolmaker, you must expect to put in about ten years of varied experience. If you have had the benefit of a four-year apprenticeship, you can arrive at top brackets within another four or five years.

You should, however, try to avoid pitfalls of narrow specialization in any one field. There is a great deal of auxiliary information to be acquired, such as blueprint reading, drawing, mathematics, and science, much of which can be gotten in evening and correspondence school as well as on the job. As a toolmaker, you may make gauges, jigs, and fixtures, or you can make dies and tools for such specialties as jewelry and watchcases. With this background, any topnotch job in the shop is within your grasp. If you have the necessary leadership traits, you can become a supervisor and eventually reach higher managerial posts such as master mechanic, superintendent, and work manager.

Jobs like these can lead to executive levels. But to get started in management the machinist must have a varied background of some years in most phases of machine shop operations as well as leadership qualities.

However, not everyone can become a toolmaker. If you wish, you may become a highly skilled machine tool operator such as a lathe hand within four to five years. Here, too, you can rise to supervisory status if you possess the necessary traits and training background. Or you can turn to inspection which now offers good opportunities to a mechanic with about five years of varied experience. If you like the production shops, with four to five years of experience you can become a set-up person on screw machines, turret lathes, milling machines, and so on. This position may also lead to managerial posts.

Another opportunity for diversification and advancement for the machinist has emerged in the development of the computerized numerical control technique as applied to the operation of machine tools. This has been mentioned in previous pages. The skilled machinist can take advantage of this.

A small but growing number of machinists have made the change from wearing a blue collar on the shop floor to a white collar in the upstairs office.

People with programming experience but no machining experience find it difficult to formulate programs for making parts the simplest and most efficient way. A former machinist said that his firsthand knowledge of machining was very valuable. He could see the operation in his mind as he transferred the specifications of a blueprint onto a program sheet from which a tape would be keypunched.

Of course, all this may be contingent on circumstances. Your first job may determine your career path. In any case, your future prospects will depend on what you desire to become, plus your experience and determination to learn all you possibly can about your job beyond the mere routine of whatever task you may be doing at the moment. The possibilities are limitless.

Our world is being changed by scientists who are creating new forms of energy and power. Yet have you ever thought how futile all these ideas would be if they were not translated into actualities by the engineers and mechanics? Even after the technicians have taken the scientists' formulas and designed machinery and equipment, the machinery still must be made by mechanics who can take the plans and actually bring them to life. In this, the machinist has played a leading role. Every atomic energy laboratory or plant has connected to it a large machine shop where toolmakers and machine specialists are kept busy turning out the equipment that makes the scientists' mathematics come to life.

OTHER INDUSTRIES

Machine shops are so intimately connected with manufacturing and production industries that a person with thorough training as a machinist may find numerous opportunities in plants outside the machine or metalworking industry. For example, because of a thorough familiarity with machines, tools, materials, and processes, a machinist might become a maintenance worker in a factory where numerous machines of all types manufacture many products. In fact, it is estimated that one fourth of the all-around machinists in the United States are employed in repairing and otherwise maintaining the mechanisms which pour out the vast array of our industrial materials. These are usually interesting jobs with a great deal of variety which pay good wages, especially in some of the more highly specialized fields, such as textiles. Similarly, our transportation systems, such as the railroads, bus lines, trucking fleets, and airlines also employ maintenance and repair machinists.

FRONT OFFICE

Machinists need not confine themselves to the actual forming of metal products. Because of their background and training, they can take off their overalls or apron, put away their tools, and go into the front office of the metalworking plant as a production manager, routing operations through the factory, expediting the work, and in general supervising all production or some of its apsects. They may also write operation sheets, indicating how parts and assemblies are to be made, specifying the operations, machines, and tools. In this case they are known as methods persons or planners. You will find many want ads for this type of worker in the newspaper.

DESIGNING

In the smaller shops with no separate designing or drafting department, the toolmakers generally do their own tool designing. As a rule, they are given a blueprint of a specific part and instructed to make a drill jig, a milling fixture, a die, or any other type of tool needed for producing the piece. They then proceed to make some sketches or drawings and build the tool in accordance with these ideas.

Larger plants, however, divide these functions and employ tool designers who make the drawings for the tools needed for production from which the machinists can then work. Because of their background, the machinists are often the ideal tool designers and many of them actually leave the shop for the drawing board. From tool designing and methods planning it is but a step to tool engineering, a most responsible planning post in manufacturing which, however, requires further technical training.

LARGE MACHINERY

There also are numerous openings for trained machinists outside the actual confines of the shop. Manufacturers of large equipment and machinery, for example, use experienced employees to erect their machinery in the field. This offers an opportunity for travel and variety. Such firms as the General Electric Corporation and Westinghouse make large steam turbines which, after testing in the plant, are disassembled, sent to the place where they are to be used (which may be anywhere in the world), and erected under the guidance of supervisors from the home plant.

These people are generally machinists who have spent many years in the manufacture of these machines. In the same manner, the Harris Corporation sends its experts or outside machinists its large printing presses. There are numerous opportunites of this nature, and if this is the type of life you would like, you can seek employment with these manufacturers of large mechanical equipment and work toward this goal.

DEMONSTRATING AND SELLING

Makers of machine tools, automatic machinery, and equipment of all sorts also employ their experts for demonstrating and servicing their products. When a machine shop purchases new machines, an employee from the vendor will come in to show how these may be operated to best advantage. Again, this employee is usually a machinist who has worked for many years making the equipment and who possesses those qualities which make her or him valuable as a representative of the company. This, too, is a job to which you can aspire if you like traveling and meeting new situations continually.

Selling is often a natural sequence to this sort of work, and many a mechanic, trained as a demonstrator or public representative, finally winds up selling the product. Of course, it takes a certain type of person for success in this field. The characteristics that make a good salesperson are not always possessed by the average shop machinist. However, if you do have these traits, there is a way open to you from the machine shop to the sales department.

All this by no means exhausts the possibilities for the well-trained machinist with a good technical background. The openings cited have been listed as possibilities to steer your thinking about the future. As an example of what can happen, a friend started his career as a machinist, became a tool designer, and then became a maintenance man with a company that distributed domestic oils and oil burner and furnace equipment. His mechanical and technical experience and certain personality traits led him into selling the equipment. He ultimately became sales manager and a partner in the business. And this is by no means a unique occurrence.

If you acquire the proper training, technical background, and work experience, you will virtually be able to chart your own advancement in the machine shop trades.

In the photo above, oil filter tops enter a stamping press via a dual conveyor system. This press operates a very sophisticated progressive die to put parts into a complete assembly. The tops are packaged for customer shipment after the assembly process. Photo: M. S. Willett, Cickeysville, Maryland, and the National Tooling and Machining Association.

CHAPTER 5

RELATED FIELDS

We have discussed the many jobs and opportunities available in metalworking and in general manufacturing for the machinist with good basic training and some varied experience. Now let's discuss some of the career possibilities in fields allied to machine shop trades.

One impression you should have from this discussion so far is the paramount need for technical knowledge if you intend to better yourself professionally. Mere manipulative skills are not enough. Technical advances are so rapid and there is so much to learn all the time that the ambitious mechanic must be continually advancing his or her education by keeping current with the trade magazines, reading technical literature, going to night school, taking correspondence courses, and so on. Going a step further, it is possible to become a technician or engineer by taking a well-planned night school course.

BECOMING AN ENGINEER OR TECHNICIAN

You may well ask how a mechanic busy all day at the bench or machine can become an engineer or technician. Even day students taking the regular four-year engineering degree find their time fully occupied. Yet it can be done; it has been done by countless machinists. Let's investigate a few ways.

If you are a graduate of a technical or academic high school, your scholastic credits will probably admit you to the night or extension division of most engineering schools, technical institutes, or junior colleges. If you have all the required credits, you can register for training in mechanical, industrial, or aeronautical engineering or technology, or in any other field in which you are interested. The school will provide you with a list of the required and elective courses you need for a degree, and you can work out a program with the help of the school's advisor. It is then up to you to apply the energy and perseverance necessary to complete the course.

Of course, it is not going to be easy. It is difficult to put in a full day at the bench or machine, grab a bite to eat, then dash off to a class in analytic geometry, mechanical lab, or mechanisms. When you finally get home, there is homework to be done; your weekends cannot be devoted entirely to leisure activities. And there is the matter of paying for the courses.

Acquiring an engineering (Bachelor's) or technology (Associate) degree might take several years. Yet, despite the obstacles, it is still worthwhile. Many machinists have followed this road to emerge as engineers or technicians with specialties in design, production, manufacturing, distribution, or some other field. They have become machine designers, plant administrators, production planners and overseers, time and motion study experts, quality control supervisors, and personnel managers.

Be sure you investigate all possibilities for continuing your education. Every urban center either has such institutions as those mentioned above or is near such schools. Look around your own neighborhood and inquire about the programs offered in nearby schools. If you want national information about what schools offer engineering courses through evening and extension programs, write to the Engineers' Council for Professional Development, 345 East 47th Street, New York, New York, 10017.

Some companies encourage their employees to continue their educations by offering them financial assistance. For example, the owner of one large machine shop asked an instructor at a vocational high school to recommend two graduates of the school's machine shop course who would be good candidates for training as all-around machinists. As an incentive for them to accept employment, they were offered financial assistance to help them work their way through evening engineering courses at a local university.

Financial assistance to pay for tuition and books also is available through scholarships, grants, and loans. Such assistance often is awarded even though the recipient may only have a part-time job. To find out about financial help, consult the guidance service of the nearest federal-state employment office or the guidance or financial aid office of the institution you wish to attend. Additionally, you may wish to consult the following for further information:

> *Scholarships, Loans, and Awards Offered by the Fifty States, District of Columbia, and Puerto Rico.* Moravia, New York: Chronicle Guidance Publications. (Published annually)
>
> Keeslar, Oreon. *Financial Aids for Higher Education.* Dubuque, Iowa: Wm. C. Brown, Publisher. (Revised periodically)
>
> Mathies, L., and E. Dixon, eds. *Scholarships, Fellowships, Grants and Loans.* Riverside, New Jersey: Macmillan Publishing, 1974.

TEACHING

Have you ever thought of a career in teaching? Probably such an idea has never crossed your mind or it has appeared to you as rather far-fetched. Yet the possibilities exist and are not too difficult to attain, as proved by the many machinists now teaching in vocational, technical, evening, and extension trade programs all over the country.

Public vocational education has come a long way since the turn of the century, and particulary since 1975. It is one of the few educational programs partly subsidized by the federal government; the federal government invests approximately $700 million each year in support of vocational education. The states and local governments invest even more—in the range of $2.5 billion annually. Today, there are nearly 20,000,000 persons enrolled in some form of trade or skills training at either secondary or post-secondary school levels.

Vocational education and skills training are expected to continue expanding in coming years. The Vocational Education Acts of 1963, 1964, and 1984 not only changed the entire structure of federally financed skills training but also allocated to the states large sums of money to help pay for this development, thereby expanding employment opportunities for trade teachers.

In addition, the new Jobs Training Partnership Act, the various antipoverty measures, and the numerous state manpower training efforts all emphasize vocational training and retraining.

The employment situation of recent years has caused many people to reexamine their career objectives with

The opportunity for clarifying instructions and methods is an essential part of training. Above, students discuss a lathe project before beginning their work. Below, students using a miniature milling machine discuss an operation with their instructor. Photos: Above, Catonsville Community College, Baltimore, Maryland; below, National Tooling and Machining Association.

the result that a great deal of interest in learning a skilled trade has been aroused; consequently, there should be no lack of openings for machine shop teachers in the years ahead.

As a rule, local boards of education do not require a shop teacher to have a college degree. A high school diploma and from five to nine years of valid and comprehensive trade experience are usually the basic requirements. The larger cities may hold examinations for trade teacher licenses which usually consist of a general written test and a practical demonstration of shop skills. The successful candidate can then be appointed to an existing school vacancy. Once on the job, he or she usually is enrolled in a state-supported teacher training course or is required to take some courses at a local university.

If you like working with young people, have had sufficient experience in the shop, and see advantages in teaching as a career, you can check with the board of education in your own locality or write for information to such urban centers as Chicago, Philadelphia, New York City, and Los Angeles which have large programs of vocational education. Write to the American Vocational Association, 2020 North 14th St. Arlington, VA 22201 for information on which localities need machine shop teachers and then get in touch with these places. If your trade experience or educational background is not yet sufficient to qualify you as a teacher, you can delay your plans but keep a teaching career in mind.

Teaching can be a most satisfactory experience. Teachers usually receive livable salaries and have work days of about six and a half hours, summer vacations of six to eight weeks, chances for advancement to supervisory or administrative positions, some form of job tenure, and pensions after a certain length of service. They also have the satisfaction of helping young people clarify their goals and start a career. Teachers employed in civil service will make no fortunes, but at least they have some security in their jobs and a large amount of time off which they can devote to developing other interests. Additionally, teachers have an opportunity to develop many satisfactory relationships with young people and the community.

SELF-EMPLOYMENT

In all our discussions concerning opportunities in the metalworking trades, we have depicted machinists as employees on wages for some firm or employer. Americans, however, by tradition and temperament, have always dreamed about and worked toward being their own bosses. For machinists, this would mean operating their own shops or businesses connected in some manner with the metal trades. However, with machinery, equipment, and labor costs so high, this choice is not an easy or simple one.

There was a time when skilled machinists could start their own shops without the expenditure of too much capital or the assumption of large debts. There's the story of a good toolmaker and blacksmith who went on his own in the early 1900s in a basement shop with a forge, an anvil, a drill press, an old lathe, some hand tools, and a great deal of energy, shrewdness, and will to succeed. When he died, he left his family one of the largest and best-equipped machine shops in New York City.

This kind of story has probably been repeated countless times in our country, and certainly as many opportunities exist now as ever before. Some sections of our country offer numerous opportunities. Young people with skill and courage can surely succeed on their own. If you are the sort of person who will never be happy until you are working for yourself and nothing will stop you, then the following information may interest you.

First, you must have sufficient all-around experience in machine shops to enable you to handle any production problems which may arise. If you lack this broad basis of practical and technical knowledge and experience, you should plan your future so as to acquire it.

This experience is absolutely necessary when you operate your own shop, because initially you will not be able to delegate your production problems on to a supervisor or someone else. The responsibility will be yours, and every bit of experience you have accumulated will be necessary to succeed in your own business.

In addition, however, you must learn something about modern business practices and problems. Production will be only half the story. If you wish to remain in business, you will have to learn how money is spent before it is made. Not only will you have to purchase materials and equipment, hire and fire employees, sell or market your products, establish financial credit, and handle a multitude of other duties, you will also have to deal with a host of governmental taxes, restrictions, and regulations.

When the toolmaker in the story opened his shop, he did not have to worry about income taxes, employee withdrawal accounts, corporation taxes, excess profit taxes, state insurance funds, unemployment insurance, social security payments, union restrictions, shop stewards, paid vacation funds for employees, or an endless number of other matters. Today all these factors have to be dealt with daily. You will also have to know something about business law, and how it affects partnerships, contracts, liens, accounts, notes, and leases. It will not be necessary for you to be an accountant, but an adequate understanding of record keeping is an asset. You should have a basic knowledge of labor law, too.

How are you going to acquire this broad background when your job keeps you busy all day? The answer lies in activities outside your job. You can take evening, extension, or correspondence courses. Watch for advertisements of such courses or inquire at your local schools, both public and private. You can acquire a certain amount of business experience on your daily job. The federal government offers many publications containing information about running your own business. You can find out about these by calling your local government documents information center.

The federal government has long been interested in the small businesses in our national economy. It has set up the Small Business Administration (SBA) which has primary responsibility to help small business ventures.

It offers free or low cost workshops at localities all over the nation where interested people can learn the fundamentals of operating a small business. There are Small Business Administration offices in all fifty states. The SBA publishes a free calendar every two months listing dates, times, and titles of courses offered at city agencies and colleges. Contact your local SBA agency or write to the Small Business Administration, Washington, D.C., 20416.

The agency also publishes numerous leaflets and pamphlets dealing with management aids for small businesses. To get information and copies, write to the Small Business Administration, P.O. Box 15434, Fort Worth, Texas 76119.

In addition to all this, the SBA, under certain conditions, will help small businesses with loans, technical assistance, and management advice. It also operates a subsidiary called the Small Business Investment Companies which will also help with finances and consulting services. For further information on this write to the Small Business Investment Companies, 512 Washington Building, Washington, D.C. 20005.

For more detailed information the following references may be of help.

>Baumback, Lawyer & Kelly. *How to Organize and Operate a Small Business.* Englewood Cliffs, N.J.: Prentice-Hall, Inc., 1973.
>
>Stevens, Mark. *How to Run Your Own Business.* New York: Simon & Schuster, 1978.

There are many ways of establishing yourself in business. If you can arrange funding, you can purchase a shop outright or buy an interest in a going concern. Of course, you will first have to make the proper inquiries as to financial standing, credits, accounts receivable, business contracts and connections, and so on. Since it would be rather unusual for a young machinist to have the kind of money necessary for this procedure, we will not pursue this any further than mentioning it.

Each of the several trade associations already mentioned publishes materials to help business owners and managers more effectively run their companies. For instance the National Tooling and Machining Association (9300 Livingston Road, Ft. Washington, MD 20744) offers a wide variety of management aids.

However, if you have invented, designed, or perfected a gadget or some sort of special equipment, tool, or device which has merit and sales possibilities, you might be able to interest enough backers to set up a shop. However, the high cost of machine tools (new or secondhand), the other necessary tools and equipment and skilled labor are going to require quite a lot of money or credit. Nevertheless, if your product has merit, you might successfully set up your own shop if you have the necessary persistence and drive.

However, some attention should be paid to protecting inventions and unique equipment or gadgets you may have designed and are proposing to manufacture. The usual method is to patent such items, but obtaining a patent is a lengthy, complicated, and sometimes costly endeavor. It usually requires a search of existing patents, special drawings as specified by the U.S. Patent

Office, writing up claims and information in accordance with regulations and other legalities, all of which should be done by a patent attorney who can do all the above and represent your interests throughout the procedures with the Patent Office. When a patent is finally granted you still have the problem of protecting it, for if it shows commercial promise others may be tempted to infringe upon it unless your lawyer initiates court proceedings to protect your patent. This can be a costly matter. Two books which can be consulted for patent information:

> Fenner, T.W. and Everett. *Inventors Handbook.* New York: Chemical Publishing Co., 1969.
>
> Kessler, H.O. & Carlisle N. *The Successful Inventor's Guide.* Englewood Cliffs, N.J.: Prentice-Hall, Inc., 1967.

For more detailed technical information on patents, write to the Commissioner of Patents, Patent Office, Washington, D.C. 20025.

In addition to all this, the federal government has created an Energy Related Inventions Program within the U.S. Department of Energy. Operated in cooperation with the National Bureau of Standards, the object of this program is to encourage individual inventors to submit their ideas for evaluation by the National Bureau of Standards. If this agency finds ideas that seem feasible and have possibilities for commercial development, it might provide development grants. These grants need not be used only for technical improvement; they can also be used for designing merchandising and marketing techniques. This agency is a flexible operation, ready to encourage and help perfect any idea that might diminish our energy crisis. An unusual aspect of the program is that it helps small business operators and individual inventors. The ideas or inventions need not be patented or even be patentable. Over 10,000 ideas and inventions have been evaluated and some have been found worthy of support.

For further information write to the Office of Inventions and Innovative Programs, CE 12, Dept. of Energy, Washington, D.C., 20585.

Some mechanics have started by setting up a few small machines, such as a bench lathe and a sensitive drill in the basement or garage of their homes. By taking on contract or subcontract work, they have managed to make a start and expand into larger commercial quarters.

If you have connections to firms or individuals from which you can secure sizable amounts of contract or subcontract work, you can get started on the strength of this. It may mean borrowing the necessary capital and living on a shoestring for a while, but if you can deliver or if you develop a specialty, you can probably succeed. For example, I know of one small shop which is doing very well making small, high-precision parts, turning these out on subcontracts from large producers of airplane engines and parts, experimental weapons, and other such highly specialized articles.

About the poorest approach is to set up a shop without any definite products or specialty in mind, trusting that the work will come in. It probably will not work out. Such an effort is very risky and most fail.

Opening a tool and die shop, a machine shop, or a production plant are not the only outlets for the machinist. For example, there was a case where two brothers, both skilled machinists started a sales agency selling and servicing certain well-known machines and tools. They were very successful. Another mechanic established a boat yard with a machine shop which kept busy reconditioning, repairing, and maintaining motor boat engines and equipment.

In another instance, a young person rented some space in a garage and set up an automobile machine shop. He and a partner installed some machines for turning brake drums, grinding valves, and the like. In a short while they were doing this type of machining for a whole group of garages and service stations and were able to rent larger, more suitable quarters. Subsequently, they purchased a crankshaft grinder and other equipment enabling them to offer a complete motor rebuilding service.

In short, there are plenty of opportunities for going into business in some branch of metalworking with good chances of success if you have the temperament, the necessary experience, some idea of how business functions, some capital and credit, the ability to take a chance, and a bit of luck. Of course, there is no denying that not all of us are suited for a business life with its ups and downs, its constant worry and drive, and the almost constant insecurity. Many of us are perfectly happy as wage earners and are certainly making our contributions and leading useful lives. So if you are considering going into business, just make sure you are the adventurous type and have the necessary skills, knowledge and information. Additional information is available in the books listed in the Appendix.

APPENDIX A

RECOMMENDED READING

Apprenticeship Past and Present. U.S. Department of Labor, Bureau of Apprenticeship and Training. Washington, D.C.

A Woman's Guide to Apprenticeship. Department of Labor, Washington, DC.

Bone, Jan. *Opportunities in Computer Aided Design and Computer Aided Manufacturing.* National Textbook Company, 4255 W. Touhy, Lincolnwood, Illinois, 60646, 1986.

Brief History of the American Labor Movement. U.S. Department of Labor, Bureau of Labor Statistics. Washington, D.C.

Career Opportunities. National Tooling and Machining Association, 9300 Livingston Road, Ft. Washington, MD 20744. (Film/videocassette available for loan or purchase.)

Career Opportunities in the Tooling and Machining Industry. National Tooling and Machining Association, 9300 Livingston Road, Ft. Washington, MD 20744. (Single copy free.)

Directory of Accredited Vocational Schools. National Association of Trade and Technical Schools, 2021 L Street N.W., Washington, D.C. 20036.

Home Study Bluebook and Directory of Private House Study Schools and Courses. National Home Study Council, 1601-18th St., Washington, D.C. 20009.

The Making of a Machinist. National Tooling and Machining Association. 9300 Livingston Road, Ft. Washington, MD 20744. (Single copy free.)

Occupational Outlook Handbook. Department of Labor. Washington, D.C. (Revised biannually.)

Pilts, Griff D. *How To Select a Private Vocational School.* Washington, D.C.: National Vocational Guidance Association.

Reuther, Victor. *The Brothers Reuther.* Boston, Mass.: Houghton, Miflin Co., 1976.

Sources of Information on Student Aid. National Education Association, Research Division, 1201-16th Street N.W., Washington, D.C. 20009 (25 cents).

Tool and Die Maker. Department of Human Resources and Development, 900 Capitol Mall, Sacramento, Cal. 95814.

The Toolmaker's Art. National Tooling and Machining Association, 9300 Livingston Road, Ft. Washington, MD 20744. (Film/videocassette available for loan or purchase.)

APPENDIX B

UNITED STATES CIVIL SERVICE REGIONS

For convenience in administration of the field service the Commission has divided the United States into regions. The following shows the names of the Commission's regional headquarters and the geographic areas served by these offices:

REGION	HEADQUARTERS	AREA SERVED
Atlanta	Atlanta Merchandise Mart 240 Peachtree Street N.W. Atlanta, Georgia 30303	Alabama, Florida, Georgia, Kentucky, Mississippi, North Carolina, South Carolina, and Tennessee.
Boston	Post Office & Courthouse Building Boston, Massachusetts 02109	Connecticut, Maine, Massachusetts, New Hampshire, Rhode Island, and Vermont.
Chicago	Main Post Office Building 433 W. Van Buren Street Chicago, Illinois 60607	Illinois, Indiana, Michigan, Minnesota, Ohio, and Wisconsin.
Dallas	1114 Commerce Street Dallas, Texas 75202	Arkansas, Louisiana, New Mexico, Oklahoma, and Texas.

Denver	Bldg. 20, Denver Federal Center Denver, Colorado 80225	Colorado, Montana, North Dakota, South Dakota, Utah, and Wyoming.
New York	New Federal Building 26 Federal Plaza New York, New York 10007	New Jersey, New York, Puerto Rico, and Virgin Islands.
Philadelphia	Customhouse 2nd & Chestnut Streets Philadelphia, Pennsylvania 19106	Delaware, Maryland, Pennsylvania, Virginia, and West Virginia.
St. Louis	1256 Federal Building 1520 Market Street St. Louis, Missouri 63103	Iowa, Kansas, Missouri, and Nebraska.
San Francisco	Federal Building, Box 36010 450 Golden Gate Avenue San Francisco, California 94102	Arizona, California, Hawaii, Nevada, and the Pacific Overseas Area.
Seattle	3004 Federal Office Bldg. 1st Avenue & Madison St. Seattle, Washington 98104	Alaska, Idaho, Oregon, and Washington.

APPENDIX C

U.S. DEPARTMENT OF LABOR BUREAU OF APPRENTICESHIP AND TRAINING

REGIONAL OFFICES

Region I, JFK Building, Room 510, Government Center, Boston, Massachusetts 02203.
Connecticut, Maine, Massachusetts, New Hampshire, Rhode Island, Vermont.

Region II, 1515 Broadway & 44th Street, Room 3731, New York, New York 10036.
New Jersey, New York, Puerto Rico, Virgin Islands.

Region III, P.O. Box 8796, Philadelphia, Pennsylvania 19101.
Delaware, Maryland, Pennsylvania, Virginia, West Virginia.

Region IV, 1371 Peachtree Street, N.E., Room 700, Atlanta, Georgia 30367.
Alabama, Florida, Georgia, Kentucky, Mississippi, North Carolina, South Carolina, Tennessee.

Region V, 230 South Dearborn Street, Room 701, Chicago, Illinois 60604.
Illinois, Indiana, Michigan, Minnesota, Ohio, Wisconsin.

Region VI, Federal Building, 525 Griffin Square, Room 858, Dallas, Texas 75202.
Arkansas, Louisiana, New Mexico, Oklahoma, Texas.

Region VII, Federal Office Building, Room 1100, 911 Walnut Street, Kansas City, Missouri 64106.
Iowa, Kansas, Missouri, Nebraska.

Region VIII, U.S. Custom House, Room 476, 721 19th Street, Denver, Colorado 80202.
Colorado, Montana, North Dakota, South Dakota, Utah, Wyoming.

Region IX, 211 Main Street, Room 343, San Francisco, California 94105
Arizona, California, Hawaii, Nevada.

Region X, Federal Office Building, Room 8018, 909 First Avenue, Seattle, Washington 98174.
Alaska, Idaho, Oregon, Washington.

STATE OFFICES

Alaska
Room E-512
Federal Building &
  Courthouse, Box 37
701 C Street
Anchorage 99513
  907/271-5035

Alabama
Berry Building
Suite 102
2017-2nd Ave., North
Birmingham 35203
  205/254-1308

Arizona
Suite 302
3221 North 16th St.
Phoenix 85016
602/241-2964

Arkansas
Room 3014
Federal Building
700 West Capitol Street
Little Rock 72201
501/378-5415

California
Room 350
211 Main Street
San Francisco 94105-1978
415/974-0556

Colorado
Room 480
U.S. Custom House
721 19th Street
Denver 80202
303/844-4793

Connecticut
Room 367
Federal Building
135 High Street
Hartford 06103
203/722-3886

Delaware
Lock Box 36
Federal Building
844 King Street
Wilmington 19801
302/573-6113

Florida
Room 3080
Hobbs Federal Building
227 North Bronough Street
Tallahassee 32301
904/681-7161

Georgia
Room 203
1371 Peachtree Street, N.E.
Atlanta 30367
404/881-4403

Hawaii
Room 5113
P.O. Box 50203
300 Ala Moana Boulevard
Honolulu 96850
808/546-7569

Idaho
Room 493
P.O. Box 006
550 West Fort St.
Boise 83724
208/334-1013

Illinois
Room 505
7222 W. Cermak Road
North Riverside 60546
312/447-0382

Indiana
Room 414
Federal Building and U.S.
　Courthouse
46 E. Ohio Street
Indianapolis 46204
317/269-7592

Iowa
Room 367
Federal Building
210 Walnut Street
Des Moines 50309
515/284-4690

Kansas
Room 370
Federal Building
444 S.E. Quincy Street
Topeka 66683
913/295-2624 (Ext. 236)

Kentucky
Room 554-C
Federal Building
600 Federal Place
Louisville 40202
502/582-5223

Louisiana
Room 925
F. Edward Hebert Building
600 South Maestri Place
New Orleans 70130
504/589-6103

Maine
Room 101-B
Federal Building—
　P.O. Box 917
68 Sewall Street
Augusta 04330
207/622-8235

Maryland
Room 1028
Charles Center—Fed. Bldg.
31 Hopkins Plaza
Baltimore 21201
301/962-2676

Massachusetts
Room E-432
JFK Federal Building
Government Center
Boston 02203
617/223-6745

Michigan
Room 657
Federal Building
231 W. Lafayette Ave.
Detroit 48226
313/226-6206

Minnesota
Room 134
Federal Building and
 U.S. Courthouse
316 Robert Street
St. Paul 55101
 612/725-7951

Mississippi
Suite 1003
Federal Building
100 West Capitol Street
Jackson 39269
 601/960-4346 or 4349

Missouri
Room 547
210 North Tucker
St. Louis 63101
 314/452-4522

Montana
Room 394—Drawer #10055
Federal Office Bldg.
301 South Park Avenue
Helena 59626-0055
 406/449-5261

Nebraska
Room 700
106 South 15th Street
Omaha 68102
 402/221-3281

Nevada
Room 311
Post Office Building
P.O. Box 1987
301 East Stewart Avenue
Las Vegas 89101
 702/388-6396

New Hampshire
Room 311
Federal Building
55 Pleasant Street
Concord 03301
 603/224-5333

New Jersey
Room 838
New Federal Building
970 Broad Street
Newark 07102
 201/645-3880

New Mexico
Room 1705
Western Bank Building
505 Marquette N.W.
Albuquerque 87102
 505/766-2398

New York
Room 810
Federal Building
North Pearl &
 Clinton Avenues
Albany 12201
 518/472-4800

North Carolina
Room 376
Federal Building
310 New Bern Avenue
Raleigh 27601
 919/755-4466

North Dakota
Room 344
New Federal Building
653 2nd Avenue, North
Fargo 58102
 701/237-5771 (Ext. 5415)

Ohio
Room 605
200 North High Street
Columbus 43215
 614/469-7375

Oklahoma
Room 526
Alfred P. Murrah
 Federal Bldg.
200 N.W. Fifth Street
Oklahoma City 73102
 405/231-4818

Oregon
Room 526
Federal Building
1220 S.W. 3rd Avenue
Portland 97204
 503/221-3157 or 3177

Pennsylvania
Room 773
Federal Building
228 Walnut Street
Harrisburg 17108
 717/782-3496

Rhode Island
100 Hartford Avenue
Providence 02909
 401/528-5068

South Carolina
Room 838
Strom Thurmond
 Federal Building
1835 Assembly Street
Columbia 29201
 803/765-5547

South Dakota
Courthouse Plaza
Room 403
300 North Dakota Ave.
Sioux Falls 57102
 605/336-2980 (Ext. 326)

Tennessee
Room 606
1720 West End Avenue
Nashville 37203
 615/749-5408

Texas
Room 2102
VA Building
2320 LaBranch Street
Houston 77004
 713/750-1696

Utah
Room 314
Post Office Building
350 South Main Street
Salt Lake City 84104
 801/524-5700

Vermont
Suite 103
Burlington Square
96 College Street
Burlington 05401
 802/951-6278

Virginia
Room 10-020
400 North 8th Street
Richmond 23240
 804/771-2488

Washington
Room 7004
Federal Office Building
909 First Avenue
Seattle 98174
 206/442-4756

West Virginia
Room 305
550 Eagan St.
Charleston 25301
 804/347-5141

Wisconsin
Room 303
Federal Center
212 E. Washington Avenue
Madison 53703
 608/264-5377

Wyoming
Room 8017
J.C. O'Mahoney
 Federal Center
P.O. Box 1126
2120 Capitol Avenue
Cheyenne 82001
 307/778-2220 (Ext. 2448)

APPENDIX D

STATE APPRENTICESHIP AGENCIES[*]

Arizona
 Apprenticeship Services
 Dept. of Economic Security
 207 East McDowell Road
 Phoenix 85004

California
 Division of Apprenticeship
  Standards
 Dept. of Industrial Relations
 525 Golden Gate Avenue
 San Francisco 94102

Colorado
 Apprenticeship Council
 1313 Sherman Street
 Denver 80203

Connecticut
 Labor Department
 Job Training & Skill
  Development
 200 Folly Brook Blvd.
 Wethersfield 06109

Delaware
 Apprenticeship Officer
 Dept. of Labor
 State Office Bldg., 6th Floor
 820 North French Street
 Wilmington 19801

District of Columbia
 D.C. Apprenticeship Council
 500 C Street, NW
 Room 241
 Washington, D.C. 20001

Florida
 Bureau of Apprenticeship
 Division of Labor
 Dept. of Labor & Employment
  Security
 1320 Executive Center Drive,
  East
 Tallahassee 32301

---

[*](Including the District of Columbia, Puerto Rico, and the Virgin Islands)

State Apprenticeship Agencies

Hawaii
Apprenticeship Division
Dept. of Labor & Industrial
  Relations
800 Punchbowl St.
Room 202
Honolulu 96813

Kansas
Apprenticeship Section
Div. of Labor-Management
  Relations and Employment
  Standards
Department of Human
  Resources
512 West 6th Street
Topeka 66603-3178

Kentucky
Apprenticeship and Training
Kentucky State Apprenticeship
  Council
620 South Third Street—
  6th Floor
Louisville 40202

Louisiana
Division of Apprenticeship
Department of Labor
5360 Florida Blvd.
Baton Rouge 70806

Maine
Maine Apprenticeship Council
Bureau of Labor Standards
State House Station No. 45
Augusta 04333

Maryland
Maryland Apprenticeship and
  Training Council
Department of Labor &
  Industry
5200 Westland Blvd.
Baltimore 21227

Massachusetts
Division of Apprentice
  Training
Department of Labor &
  Industries
Leverett Saltonstan Bldg.
100 Cambridge Street
Boston 02202

Minnesota
Division of Voluntary
  Apprenticeship
Department of Labor &
  Industry
444 Lafayette Road
St. Paul 55101

Montana
Apprenticeship Bureau,
Dept. of Labor & Industry
Lockey & Roberts Streets
2nd Floor
Helena 59620

Nevada
Department of Labor
Capitol Building,
Room 601
505 East King Street
Carson City 89710

New Hampshire
Commission of Labor
Department of Labor
19 Pillsbury Street
Concord 03301

New Mexico
New Mexico State
Apprenticeship Council
Labor and Industrial
Commission
2340 Menaul Street, Suite 212
Albuquerque 87107

New York
Apprentice Training
Department of Labor
The Campus, Building 12
Room 428
Albany 12240

North Carolina
Apprenticeship Division
Department of Labor
4 West Edenton Street
Raleigh 27601

Ohio
Ohio State Apprenticeship
Council
Department of Industrial
Relations
Room 2290
2323 W. 5th Street
Columbus 43215

Oregon
Apprenticeship and Training
Division
1400 S.W. Fifth Street
Portland 97201

Pennsylvania
Pennsylvania Apprenticeship
and Training Council
Department of Labor &
Industry
7th & Forster Streets
Room 1618
Harrisburg 17120

Puerto Rico
Apprenticeship Division
Department of Labor &
Human Rights
GPO Box 4452
San Juan 00936

Rhode Island
Rhode Island Apprenticeship
Council
Department of Labor
220 Elmwood Avenue
Providence 02907

Vermont
Vermont Apprenticeship
Council
Department of Labor and
Industry
120 State Street
Montpelier 05602

Virginia
  Division of Apprenticeship
    Training
  Department of Labor
  205 N. 4th Street
  P.O. Box 12064
  Richmond 23219

Virgin Islands
  Division of Apprenticeship
    and Training
  Department of Labor
  Christiansted, St. Croix 00820

Washington
  Apprenticeship and Training
    Division
  Department of Labor and
    Industries
  605-11th Ave. SE
  Olympia 98504

Wisconsin
  State of Wisconsin, DILHR
  Employment & Training
    Division
  Bureau of Apprenticeship
    Standards
  201 E. Washington Ave.,
    Rm. 211-X
  P.O. Box 7972
  Madison, WI 53707

APPENDIX E

PROFESSIONAL SOCIETIES, NATIONAL AND LOCAL TRADE ASSOCIATIONS, AND LABOR UNIONS

PROFESSIONAL SOCIETIES:

American Die Casting Institute
2340 Des Plaines Avenue
Des Plaines, IL 60018

American Metal Stamping Association
27027 Chardon Road
Richmond Heights, OH 44143

American Society of Manufacturing Engineers
One SME Drive
Dearborn, MI 48128

American Society of Mechanical Engineers
345 East 17th Street
New York, NY 10017

American Society for Metals
Metals Park, Ohio 44073

American Vocational Association
2020 North 14th Street
Arlington, VA 22201

Chamber of Commerce of the United States
1615 H Street N.W.
Washington, D.C. 20006

National Education Association of the United States
1201 16th Street NW
Washington, DC 20036

National Screw Machine Products Association
6700 West Snowville Road
Brecksville, OH 44141

National Vocational Guidance Association
5999 Stevenson Avenue
Alexandria, VA 22304

The Society of the Plastics Industry
355 Lexington Avenue
New York, NY 10017

TRADE ASSOCIATIONS

The National Association of Manufacturers
1776 F Street N.W.
Washington, D.C. 20006

National Association of Trade & Technical Schools
2021 K Street N.W., Suite 315
Washington, D.C. 20006

National Machine Tool Builders Association
7901 Westpark Drive
McLean, Virginia 22102

National Tooling and Machining Association
9300 Livingston Road
Ft. Washington, MD 20744

Tooling and Manufacturing Assn.
1177 S. Dee Road
Park Ridge, Illinois 60068

LABOR UNIONS

International Association of Machinists and Aerospace
 Workers
1300 Connecticut Avenue NW
Washington, DC 20036

International Union of Allied Industrial Workers of America
3520 West Oklahoma Avenue
Milwaukee, WI 53215

International Union of Electronic, Electrical, Technical
 Salaried and Machine Workers
1126 16th Street
Washington, DC 20036

HD
8039
.M52
U59
1986

11.95

HD
8039
.M52
U59

1986